Witi Ihim
A Changing Vision

The University of Otago Press
TE WHENUA SERIES
brings together works by and about people for whom the countries of the Pacific region are their home.

TE WHENUA in Maori means the land, country, ground; also placenta, afterbirth.

OTHER TITLES IN THIS SERIES:

Ruth Dallas
CURVED HORIZON: AN AUTOBIOGRAPHY

Lawrence Jones
BARBED WIRE AND MIRRORS: ESSAYS ON NEW ZEALAND PROSE

Erich Kolig
THE NOONKANBAH STORY: PROFILE OF AN ABORIGINAL COMMUNITY

Heather Murray
DOUBLE LIVES: WOMEN IN THE STORIES OF KATHERINE MANSFIELD

Jeffrey Sissons
TE WAIMANA/THE SPRING OF MANA: TUHOE HISTORY AND THE COLONIAL ENCOUNTER

Agathe Thornton
MAORI ORAL LITERATURE AS SEEN BY A CLASSICIST

Other titles in the offshoot series TE WHENUA/TE REO THE LAND/THE LANGUAGE:

Ray Harlow
A Name and Word Index to NGĀ MAHI A NGĀ TŪPUNA

FORTHCOMING:

Simon Rae
BREATH BECOMES THE WIND: OLD AND NEW IN KARO RELIGION

Witi Ihimaera:
A Changing Vision

by Umelo Ojinmah

TE WHENUA SERIES NO.7
PACIFIC PEOPLE, LAND AND LITERATURE

UNIVERSITY OF OTAGO PRESS

This book was produced with the assistance
of the Computing Services Centre, University of Otago,
typeset by Alpha Typesetting, Dunedin, and
printed by the University Printery

The paper used is Bookprint Hi-Bulk paper (95 gsm)
which is of a suitable quality to meet the Interim
Australian Standard AS 4003 (Int)-1992 for the
Permanence of uncoated paper and paperboard

Cover design by Jenny Cooper
Front cover photograph by Peter Coates

The publishers gratefully acknowledge the contributions
of the photographers named in the list of illustrations,
and apologize for those instances where the copyright
holders were not able to be contacted for their permission,
or not known and named

ISBN 0 908569 57 2

National Library of New Zealand
Cataloguing-in-Publication data

Ojinmah, Umelo R. (Umelo Reubens), 1954-
Witi Ihimaera : a changing vision / Umelo Ojinmah. Dunedin, N.Z. :
University of Otago Press, 1993.
1 v. (Te Whenua series, 0114-4995 ; no. 7)
Includes bibliographical references.
ISBN 0-908569-57-2 (pbk.) : $24.95
1. Ihimaera, Witi, 1944- --Criticism and interpretation. 2. English
literature--Maori authors--History and criticism. 3. Authors, New
Zealand--20th century--History and criticism. I. Title. II. Series:
Whenua series ; no. 7.
NZ823.2 zbn92-100715

Published 1993 by the University of Otago Press
Box 56 Dunedin New Zealand
Fax: (03) 479 8362

For Simbo

CONTENTS

Illustrations

All the illustrations appear between pages 10 and 11. The photographers are acknowledged here.

1. Witi with his paternal grandmother, Teria Pere, about 1947, Gisborne.
2. With his father, Te Haa, at Rongopai meeting house, Waituhi, 1985. [Peter Coates]
3. Paintings inside Rongopai, Waituhi. [Peter Coates]
4. Te Haa with David Heap (Witi's publisher for *The Matriarch*) outside Rongopai, 1987. [Susan Heap]
5. External painting, Rongopai, Waituhi. [Peter Coates]
6. Waituhi landscape, near where Hine Te Ariki lived. [Peter Coates]
7. With his daughters on the marae at Waituhi, 1986. [*Gisborne Herald*]
8. Witi's parents, Julia and Tom Smiler (Te Haa Ihimaera), 1988.
9. With Ngahuia Te Awekotuku at the first Maori Writers and Artists Conference, Te Kaha, 1973. [John Miller]
10. With composer Ross Harris at a rehearsal of their opera, *Waituhi: The Life of the Village*, based on Witi's novel, *Whanau*. Directed by Adrian Kiernander, *Waituhi* premièred in Wellington in 1984. [Robert Axford]
11. Rehearsal of *Waituhi*, with musical director Ross Harris, director Adrian Kiernander (on his left), Witi and members of the company. [Robert Axford]
12. Marjorie Roes (left) as Maka and Harata Solomon as Mere in *Waituhi*. The set was designed by Para Matchitt. [Robert Axford]
13. From left, Pou Temara as Paora, Nathan or Tane Grey as his mokopuna, Pene; Matira Taikato as Annie Jackson and Leah Couch as Rose in *Waituhi*. [Robert Axford]
14. The Ihimaera family in the 1940s: Witi's grandmother and father at left back.
15. Some of the Ihimaera clan, 1991; Witi at centre, wearing a black shirt. [Vicki Lewis]

Foreword

This book has its origins in Dr Ojinmah's Ph.D. thesis, a comparative study of Witi Ihimaera and Chinua Achebe as post-colonial writers. Umelo Ojinmah had come to the University of Otago as a private graduate student in 1986, determined to write a thesis making cross-cultural comparisons, and soon settled on Ihimaera and Achebe as suitable writers because of their similar conscious roles as cultural spokespeople and social critics. This book is a development from the section of the thesis dealing with Ihimaera's work.

Although Achebe's work is not dealt with in the book, it is there as a silent presence, as part of the Nigerian perspective from which Dr Ojinmah views Ihimaera. Michael Neill has written that to approach New Zealand from the perspective of third-world post-colonial literature is "to subject oneself to the shock of painful and unexpected recognitions; it is to begin to see this country and its past in a new light—to begin a lesson in history and geography from which one's sense of self, of where one stands, will emerge changed".[1] It is such a perspective that this book offers us. One aspect of that perspective is the belief, so evident in Achebe's critical essays, that literature is representational and that the writer has a social role to play as reality instructor. Thc post-structural critical games of Paris and New Haven (not to speak of Irvine or North Carolina) are not for Dr Ojinmah; he meets Ihimaera on the writer's own ground of social concern and criticises the work in terms of the writer's own stated goals.

Another aspect of Dr Ojinmah's Nigerian perspective is his view of New Zealand as a post-colonial settler society. The post-colonial status, with its attendant problems of urban drift and cultural dislocation of indigenous peoples, it shares with Nigeria, while the special problems of a settler society, with the indigenous people a minority, differentiate it. Dr Ojinmah is aware of both the similarities and the differences in his analysis of the development of Ihimaera's "bicultural vision", that painful attempt to find a narrow ridge of biculturalism between the abysses of assimilation and separatism.

This is a book for both Maori and Pakeha readers, as Ihimaera's own work is offered both to Pakeha and to Maori, young and old — to educate the young and to honour the elders and ancestors in their Maoritanga. It pursues, as do Ihimaera's fiction and his collections and co-editions of Maori writing (*Into the World of Light*, and *Te Ao Marama*) the simple aim voiced by Granny Rita in Patricia Grace's story, "Parade": "To show others who we are".[2] What is different about this book is that "we" in this instance refers also to indigenous people in societies other than our own.

The analysis is very much an interim report, for Ihimaera's career is still in process. Indeed, his most recent work of fiction, *Dear Miss Mansfield*, appeared too late for inclusion in this study. That work, itself a very "bicultural" gesture, does not really modify the vision presented in this book; however, *Tiana*, the anticipated sequel to *The Matriarch*, may well come to represent the next stage in the process that Dr Ojinmah has charted.

In the mean time, in the wake of a troubled sesquicentennial year, with all of the ambivalent feelings it aroused, Dr Ojinmah's analysis is timely and useful, a critique of an important body of work from an unexpected and relevant perspective.

Lawrence Jones
University of Otago
1993

Acknowledgements

I wish to thank the Department of English, University of Otago, for the grant that started it all, and particularly Associate Professor Lawrence Jones, for his friendship and personal interest, help and input into the work, for his expertise in the field and especially for pointing out certain errors of cultural assumption on my part. My thanks also go to Professor A. G. Fox, Professor Colin Gibson and the staff of the English Department. Special thanks are due to the 1990 Commission and Dunedin Commissioner, Robert Montgomery, and to Dr Helen Watson White and the University of Otago Press for making the publication of this book possible.

ACKNOWLEDGEMENTS

1

♠♥♠

Ihimaera and the Maori Perspective

Much has been said of Bill Pearson's 1969 essay "The Maori and Literature 1938–65" as being the catalyst that turned Witi Ihimaera into a writer, but it was not the only one.[1] Richard Corballis and Simon Garrett have identified four important factors that contributed to Ihimaera becoming a writer: in addition to Pearson's essay, which mentioned that there were still no Maori novelists or dramatists, they noted the encouragement of Jane Cleghorn, who later became Witi's wife, and his personal interest in telling stories.[2] As Pearson himself states in a later essay: "I have no doubt that Witi Ihimaera would have started writing sooner or later."[3]

Ihimaera himself recalls "an early interest in telling and writing stories for his little sisters", as Corballis and Garrett relate:

> One recollection he has is of writing stories across the whole wall of his room at the family farm at Whakarau. He would wake up from a dream and look round for a place to write down its details while they were still fresh. Although his mother pinned sheets of paper to the wall, these did not always accommodate what he wanted to write down, and he would stray on to the wallpaper. Written in the dark, these lines were not always straight. Nevertheless, when his room was redecorated, Witi urged his mother to

> preserve the old wallpaper because all his "good ideas" were written on it.[4]

But most especially, "Ihimaera cites the fact that he is a Maori as an important element in his ambition to become a writer. Writing was to be his way of doing something for the Maori people, he would express how it felt to be Maori to them as well as to the Pakeha."[5] The importance of this aspect of his motivation and inspiration is underscored by the fact that Ihimaera has reiterated this commitment so very often, both in his fiction and essays:

> My first priority is to the young Maori, the ones who have suffered most with the erosion of the Maori map, the ones who are Maori by colour but who have no emotional identity as Maori. My second priority is the Pakeha—he must understand his Maori heritage, must understand that cultural difference is not a bad thing and that, in spite of the difference, he can incorporate the Maori vision of life into his own personality. Thirdly, I write for all New Zealanders to make them aware of the tremendous value of Maori culture and the tragedy for them should they continue to disregard this part of their dual heritage.[6]

Writing was thus, for Ihimaera, a way of redressing the dearth of Maori voices on contemporary issues of relevance to Maori, a way of bringing the Maori culture "into the world of light",[7] and most importantly, his way of saying to both the Pakeha and the world—here we are, this is us, Maori.

Critics such as John Beston have noted that Ihimaera "grew up during the time of quickest change in Maori life."[8] Ihimaera, Beston says, "was old enough either to realize at the time what was happening or to observe the changes and interpret them in later years."[9] What Ihimaera observed was a migration of Maori from their rural and agriculturally based communities to the urban areas; an inversion in the ratio of rural to urban Maori, and an attendant cultural discontinuity. Beston remarks that at the time Ihimaera was born, about eighty-five percent of Maori still lived in rural areas and that most were agricultural and seasonal workers. But after the Second World War, they began to migrate to the urban centres. Between 1970 and 1975 startling changes occurred: the proportion of Maori living in the rural areas and the cities was inversed from a sixty percent rural/forty percent urban ratio in 1970 to a thirty percent rural/seventy percent urban ratio in 1975.[10]

Ihimaera thus witnessed the gradual assimilation of the Maori into the dominant Pakeha culture, but is aware that while "the Maori [was becoming] increasingly integrated into the Pakeha way of life, that integration has always been a one-way process."[11] Also relevant in Beston's opinion is that "the severing of the strong ties binding the Maori to their tribal lands when they moved to the cities has been the major threat to their cultural identity."[12] This unwelcome development accounts for Ihimaera's initial bid to use his writing to "encourage Maori people to resist further change in the villages" which hold "the spirit of Maoritanga" and "the heart of [their] culture."[13] It is this response and the fact that, as Ihimaera says, the life he writes about has its roots in the earth that give rise to the "pastoral" quality of the early works. He classes his early works with what he calls the pastoral tradition of written Maori literature because they lack anger and political thought and are tender, unabashedly lyrical evocations of a world that once was.

When one considers Ihimaera's written works, however, it becomes obvious that he has a distinctive analysis which incorporates a contemporary Maori point of view. Ihimaera, on the one hand, has been accused by Maori activists of being an "uncle Tom", a "brown Pakeha", and of expressing his masters' (Pakeha) voice instead of a Maori one. His stories, Bill Pearson notes, "have disappointed some Maori activists who think writing by Maori should advance the cause of Maori rights: 'middle-class Maori', 'Pakeha pet', are some of the names he has been called."[14] Atareta Poananga, one of the most vocal Maori critics of Ihimaera's writings, says of Ihimaera: "He is a representative of the ... apologists for the white man."[15] On the other hand, he has also been upbraided both by Pakeha and by Maori elders for being vocal. Pakeha have chided him for voicing Maori disenchantments, and threatened his career. As Poananga said in an interview with Nicola Legat of *Metro*, Ihimaera "was told he could be fired too because he had also gone public."[16] Maori elders, for their part, have been upset that he was exposing the sacredness of Maori ways to profane gaze: "They felt putting such things into print was a sacred matter, a tapu matter."[17] Maintaining a balance between these three groups has entailed a kind of tightrope walking for Ihimaera.

He is a socially conscious writer in the vein defined by David Cook: "The socially conscious writer does not set to work in a vacuum, but urges his society from what it is towards what it might be."[18] This social consciousness and his avowed aim to make Pakeha New Zealanders aware of their "other" heritage have informed Ihimaera's view all along. While some of his opinions, particularly on biculturalism, have come under a barrage of criticism from Maori nationalists who claim that it is a "Pakeha co-optive strategy ... assimilation in another guise," Ihimaera firmly believes that it is the only viable option left for the Maori.[19] He says:

> If we don't establish a sense of biculturalism in New Zealand now, which is an equality between Maori and European in New Zealand, then either New Zealand will be completely mono-cultural, or else there will be another revolution or retaliation like Te Kooti's and after it there will be another backlash against the Maori people. In both cases, Maoris will lose.[20]

He uses his fiction as a means of persuasively articulating his concept of biculturalism which, further to the above definition, he sees as the ability of either a Maori or Pakeha New Zealander to bestride both worlds without feeling a stranger in either. Ihimaera's fiction analyses both the consequences of colonization and the post-colonial tensions from a Maori perspective. His views hinge upon his perception of an ironic sense of the gap between the dreams of Maori to make it in the Pakeha world and of Maori parents to give their children a better future, and the reality of frustrated hopes, urban alienation, and family disintegration as revealed by the course of history. In examining the origins and manifestations of these post-colonial tensions, from the advent of the Pakeha, through the settler period and the period of initial Maori drift to the city until the present day, his fiction shows a marked shift in attitude. From having a non-activist stance, Ihimaera has become more militant as he probes the historical causes of the present reality and the Maori predicament.

His fiction conveys a message which fervently urges biculturalism; however, in conveying this message, Ihimaera constructs an account of the historical origins of the present predicament from a Maori vantage point that is polemical. Believing that there are always two sides to any story, he is concerned to present a Maori one to correct and counterbalance traditional Pakeha versions that he considers partial and biased.

With the publication of *Pounamu, Pounamu* in 1972, Witi Ihimaera began to raise some contemporary issues in Maori consciousness for analysis, the predominant one being the need to convey the Maori heritage to the rest of the world, from a Maori perspective. Considering that the New Zealand literary landscape has been dominated by Pakeha writers, who write both on Pakeha and Maori issues, Ihimaera, in his novels (*Tangi*, published in 1973, *Whanau*, published in 1974, and *The Matriarch*, published in 1986) in his book of short stories (*The New Net Goes Fishing*, published in 1977), and in his most recent novel *The Whale Rider*, published in 1987, has sought to present a Maori insight into some of these contemporary issues. Ihimaera's distinctive analysis of issues such as Maori alienation and land problems aims at enhancing this comprehension of what it means to be Maori in post-colonial New Zealand. As Ihimaera acknowledges, "conveying this heritage through writing has not been very easy."[21] Nevertheless, he believes that his social consciousness has been the main springboard of his artistic creativity. As has been mentioned, Ihimaera started writing to rectify the dearth of Maori writing, spurred on by Bill Pearson's comment that there were still no Maori novelists or playwrights. In rectifying this anomaly, he has been motivated by the desire to make an authentic Maori world view comprehensible both to young urban Maori and to Pakeha.

His other motivation, as also noted, has been his vision of a bicultural New Zealand, and his aim to make the Pakeha realise that there are positive aspects of the cultural differences that exist in New Zealand. This explains why he has been very preoccupied in reconstructing a view of history that is Maori. It is a tribute to his social consciousness that when, in 1975, he felt that in his bid to fulfil this social obligation he had created a stereotype Maori which is at variance with contemporary reality, he made himself stop writing for a time:

> I could not, in all conscience, allow people ever to consider my work was the definitive portrayal of the world of the Maori. In my attempts to help, I considered I had created a stereotype. Of warm caring relationships. Of a people who lived in rural communities. But what was the reality? The reality of 1975 was a hardening of attitudes on both sides. Of inflexibility. Of infighting.[22]

Ihimaera's changing attitude has reflected this social consciousness. In the earlier fictions, *Pounamu, Pounamu*, *Tangi*, and *Whanau*, there is a pronounced restraint; Ihimaera had held firmly to his belief in promoting biculturalism through a non-activist style of writing, saying: "My way is with the pen; others of my people use more forceful methods." And in spite of very severe criticism from Maori activists such as Atareta Poananga, Ihimaera has maintained: "Mine is not essentially an activist approach". He has been accused, he says, of "not being 'political' enough, or critical enough of our Pakeha-dominated society or hitting hard enough at the very real social, economic, legal and other problems facing the Maori people today."[23]

With the publication of *The New Net Goes Fishing* in 1977, his *New Zealand Listener* editorials "The Maori Landscape" and "The Maori Affairs Syndrome" written for the issues of 30 July 1977 and 27 August 1977, and with publication of *The Matriarch* in 1986, it became obvious that Ihimaera was progressively becoming more militant. From creating a character like Hepa Walker, who shows indignation at the constant moaning and pointing of accusatory fingers by radical Maori activists, Ihimaera has moved to creating fiery characters such as Api in "Clenched Fist" and "Tent on the Home Ground." Of Hepa Walker, Ihimaera had written:

> Not having experienced overt discrimination, he finds it hard to believe that it does exist. What's more, he is actually embarrassed by it .... As far as he is concerned the problems are social ones, not racial at all. Holding this view, Hepa is therefore puzzled by the rise of the young Maori radicals. He does not mind too much when they point out areas where social adjustments are necessary, but he is enraged at the indiscriminate way in which they apportion the blame. You'd think they would know better than to accuse the Pakeha for all their "problems" or to say that these are due to a White racist system. Always ready to blame somebody for their ills, that's their trouble. (*Whanau*, pp. 91–2)

There is an authorial ambivalence implied in the characterisations of Hepa Walker and Api which will be looked into in a later chapter, but even George, despite his initial rebuttal of Api's accusation against the system as racist, ends up joining Api and his friends when he comes face to face with racism directed at another Maori. Artemis Mahana, the matriarch, exhorts her grandson Tamatea time after time not to trust the Pakeha:

> I have taught you to be a Maori and to fight in a Maori way. But there is another lesson which you must learn, one which my great-uncle taught me when I was a child. He sent me away from this place to another across the sea. I did not understand then, but I did when I returned .... I have taught you to fight the Pakeha. But I had forgotten that to fight the Pakeha you must learn to be like him. You must become a Pakeha, think like him, act like him and, when you know you are in his image then turn your knowledge to his destruction. (*The Matriarch*, p. 427)

These radical characterisations, coupled with Ihimaera's extra-literary activities noted above, indicate a changed attitude.[24] It is noteworthy however that, despite this changed attitude, Ihimaera still recognises New Zealand's need for a bicultural society, and consistently upholds this view.

Although Ihimaera has written a book of essays, *Maori*,[25] and has co-edited an anthology of Maori writings, *Into the World of Light*,[26] it is through his fiction that he most persuasively articulates his view. His acknowledgement of the tremendous strides which the Maori have made in the post-colonial era notwithstanding, Ihimaera lays bare through the medium of his fiction the deep gap between the dreams and aspirations of Maori and the reality of their situation.

In this first section I shall trace Ihimaera's concept of "bicultural integration" or "biculturalism", which has come to mean different things to different people. While to many Maori the concept has come to mean equal opportunity for everyone, some have seen it as the ability for the Maori to live in both Maori and Pakeha worlds — to know their Maori culture and still be able to live and operate in the Pakeha culture—and for the Pakeha, to know and appreciate the Maori culture as well as their own. Maori believe that their world has been changed with the coming of the Pakeha and that as it now exists it is in the image of the Pakeha; that is why they must press, in the context of biculturalism, for a restitution of the Maori point of view. Ihimaera's definition of the concept as an equality between Maori and European in New Zealand, and also as the ability to reconcile Maori and Pakeha cultural values without being alienated in either world, is an attempt to harmonise all the existing definitions, and this study would evaluate his subsequent struggles to define, develop, and defend the concept.[27]

In looking at the development of this concept of biculturalism I shall structure my argument chronologically according to the different phases in Ihimaera's development as a writer: the "pastoral phase", which will deal with his earliest works, *Pounamu, Pounamu* and *Tangi*, and the initial desire to capture the Maori heritage and the world that was; the "transitional phase", which will deal with *Whanau*, showing the rural decline and his awareness of the problems of urban migration; and the "political phase", which will deal with *The New Net Goes Fishing*, the Turnbull Lectures, the *Listener* editorials, *The Matriarch*, *The Whale Rider*, and after. I shall also deal with Ihimaera's view of the influence of the historical background on the later Maori dream, showing that the dream itself was initially a reaction to Maori disenchantment at the lack of justice in the early relationship between Maori and Pakeha. I shall, in the course of this, analyse Ihimaera's depiction of present Maori disillusionment at the shattering of that dream, showing his change of attitude, and the ambivalence implicit in this attitude. It will also be made apparent that the tensions inherent in some of his characters arise from the fact that these characters are often nearly as inextricably committed to Pakeha values as they are to Maori ones.

In dealing with his views as they relate to the development of his concept of biculturalism I shall be following the chronological order in which his works were written. However, the analyses of the historical background will not follow this chronological order because Ihimaera did not deal with the earlier history until his views had become more radical, so that, in some cases, his later writings actually provide a wider context in which to place the earlier ones. Moreover, in dealing with his total view of the Maori post-colonial situation, it is useful to analyse his views and perspective on the historical background, which can be gleaned most fully from *The Matriarch*, a novel that also gives the clearest indication of his new radical stance. However, *The Matriarch* is, more than anything, a work of fiction. In spite of the polemical nature of the historical perspective already mentioned, it contains an ambivalent attitude that complicates such issues as biculturalism and the demands of Maoritanga.

In a later chapter, I intend to use *The Matriarch* to elucidate Ihimaera's perspective on some of the accepted historical notions as indicated above, as well as to illustrate his changing attitude. However, Ihimaera's ambivalence, which is very pronounced both in his depiction of character and in his narrative, will be treated along with his changing development of the concept of biculturalism.

1. Witi with his paternal grandmother, Teria Pere, about 1947, Gisborne.

2. With his father, Te Haa, at Rongopai meeting house, Waituhi, 1985.

3. Paintings inside Rongopai, Waituhi.

4. Te Haa with David Heap (Witi's publisher for *The Matriarch*) outside Rongopai, 1987.

5. External painting, Rongopai, Waituhi.

6. Waituhi landscape, near where Hine Te Ariki lived.

7. With his daughters on the marae at Waituhi, 1986.

8. Witi's parents, Julia and Tom Smiler (Te Haa Ihimaera), 1988.

9. With Ngahuia Te Awekotuku at the first Maori Writers and Artists Conference, Te Kaha, 1973.

10. With composer Ross Harris at a rehearsal of their opera, *Waituhi: The Life of the Village*, based on Witi's novel, *Whanau*. Directed by Adrian Kiernander, *Waituhi* premièred in Wellington in 1984.

12. Marjorie Roes (left) as Maka and Harata Solomon as Mere in *Waituhi*. The set was designed by Para Matchitt.

13. From left, Pou Temara as Paora, Nathan or Tane Grey as his mokopuna, Pene; Matira Taikato as Annie Jackson and Leah Couch as Rose in *Waituhi*.

14. The Ihimaera family in the 1940s: Witi's grandmother and father at left back.

15. Some of the Ihimaera clan, 1991; Witi at centre, wearing a black shirt.

2

♣♦♣

From Pastoral to Political:
A Changing Way of Life

The Pastoral Phase

Pounamu, Pounamu, "the first collection of short stories by a Maori writer to be published,"[1] was intended by Ihimaera to be an "offering from the Maori side" both to young urban Maori alienated from their culture, and to Pakeha who do not know the Maori part of their heritage, in the hope that the pastoral life it depicts and the values it represents will never be lost. For a culture that had no tradition of written literature, and which was reluctant to expose its tradition and cultural values to public gaze because "putting such things into print was a sacred matter, a tapu matter",[2] Ihimaera's *Pounamu, Pounamu* was a trail-blazer. It was also Ihimaera's "feelers", and like the delicate feelers of a snail had to be flicked cautiously, to break the fragile barriers between what was permissible by tradition for "outsiders" to know and read about, and what was taboo. The dilemma was that, concerned as Ihimaera was with the preservation of the culture which he saw disappearing all around him, he had to be conscious of the reticence of tribal elders, and therefore selective as to what aspects of the "tale of the tribe" could be told without offending tribal sensibilities.

The recurrent concern of Ihimaera's fiction, as Bill Pearson notes, is "cultural identity crisis, provoked by the rapid shift of Maori to the cities and the passing of the old spiritually relaxed, emotionally assured way of life that had prevailed in villages for half a century or more, involving the personal sustenance and obligations provided by the extended family, mutual aid, and a sense of fullness of living."[3] *Pounamu, Pounamu* deals with family and village interactions and aroha, and celebrates Maori culture as a living thing. Ihimaera, talking to John Beston, says that *pounamu* symbolised the preciousness of Maori culture and that he used greenstone "in association with the rural part of *Pounamu, Pounamu*" to signify "Maori life in its good old days."[4] The rural setting of *Pounamu, Pounamu* and its idyllic nature is therefore in consonance with Ihimaera's aim of showing urban young Maori and Pakeha what it is that they are missing. He says in the same interview that the spirit of Maoritanga is most alive in rural areas.

A dominant theme in the early stories contained in *Pounamu, Pounamu* is "the irrepressible spirit of the Maori community" and the evocation of the communal spirit which sustains the culture.[5] Richard Corballis and Simon Garrett have analysed the function of games in both "A Game of Cards" and "Beginning of the Tournament" as a means of bringing the people together.[6] To the characters in "A Game of Cards", the game itself is not as important as the bickering:

> If there was nobody to play with her, she'd always play patience .... She used to try to teach me some of the games, but I wasn't very interested, and I didn't yell and shout at her like the women did. She liked the bickering. (*Pounamu, Pounamu*, p. 3)

For these old women, as for Maori of their generation, the cultural discontinuity that was developing between them and their descendants meant that any game or gathering afforded them an excuse to try and stem the tide, by endeavouring to sustain the communal spirit, the feeling of oneness. The narrator explains to his Pakeha friend in "Beginning of the Tournament" that:

> The game *is* important, but it's meeting together that's more important. Meeting together and laughing together and having fun together. For a few days each year we meet each other. We might never meet again until the next year. So we make the most of these days .... But even having just this little time together is good, Jerry. This is a tournament, yes; but more than that, it's the gathering of the family. (*Pounamu, Pounamu*, pp. 12–13)

The essentiality of "the gathering of the family" and Ihimaera's concern for a retention of Maoritanga has to be set against the backdrop of Maori problems of the time. As already noted, Ihimaera began writing at a "time of the whirlwinds", as he terms it.[7] The future for Maori culture seemed bleak, and the spirit of Maoritanga, *whanaungatanga* and *manaakitanga*[8] were all under assault by the prevalent new wave of individualism which the Pakeha-dominated society and urban migration were fostering. It then was necessary that the people use any opportunities they had of gathering together to renew and freshen these cultural links and bonds. Ihimaera writes from a premise that before the advent of the Pakeha, the cohesion and intra-communal bonds within Maori tribal and extended families were tight, with everyone within the family acting as their brothers' keepers. He sees this quality as being most evident in the villages which, he shows in stories such as "Fire on Greenstone", hold the heart of Maori culture:

> When my Nanny Miro died, her husband, my Nanny Tama, stayed alone in their old homestead .... The people of the whanau would often visit him, bringing with them their crates of beer, and they would sing songs and talk about the old days with him. Nanny Tama liked that. (*Pounamu, Pounamu*, p. 33)

The needs of the elderly, both material and spiritual comforts, are provided for by the young: "—That was

Joe Baker .... He brought your Nanny some kainga kopiro" (*Pounamu, Pounamu*, p. 37). The elders are in turn expected, both by society and by the young, to provide guidance and to inculcate a sense of cultural awareness, propriety, and traditional values in the young: "He nodded his head. Then his eyes twinkled. He motioned me to a cupboard and brought out a wakahuia, a small carved box. —You remember this? he asked" (p. 37).

Through such stories as "The Makutu on Mrs Jones" and "One Summer Morning", Ihimaera explores the concerns, gossip, and interactions that give meaning to rural existence. Ihimaera's balanced handling of the parries and ripostes between Mrs Jones and Mr Hohepa inclines one to Corballis and Garrett's interpretation that the story "is really also about a game—a sex-game." [9] This reading is heightened, not only by the circumstances of Tawhai's narration of the story, as Garrett and Corballis note, but also by Ihimaera's comment that the other women could see "behind [Mrs Jones'] bluff and cheekiness to the lonely woman inside" (*Pounamu, Pounamu*, p. 16). If the women could see this, certainly the men also could, given Ihimaera's emphasis on Mrs Jones' attractiveness and desirability:

> She'd still been in her thirties when her husband had died, and the men hadn't even let him be dead a respectable time before they'd started making a play for her .... The trouble was that she was such a damned handsome woman and had so much spirit, that men found her irresistible. (*Pounamu, Pounamu*, p. 16)

But more important is the fact that, despite the general flirting of the men with her, there exists a spirit of camaraderie even with the women who did not find her a threat to their marriage, the narrator stating that "around the pa, she was very popular .... Because of her attitude, the women weren't at all jealous of her" (p. 16).

While Hema in "One Summer Morning" agonises about the chores that a thirteen-year-old "recently become man" in a family of girls has to perform, and the fact that he is only "five foot two and a quarter inches", he however admits that life on the farm is "a good life" (*Pounamu, Pounamu*, p. 86). At the same time, he complains bitterly:

> A young boy like him, stuck out in the sticks while everybody else in the world must be having a good time in their neat city apartments and going on round-the-world cruises .... What a dump! (*Pounamu, Pounamu*, p. 72)

Considering Hema's sustained moans about the hardship that rural existence involves, the admission of its good aspect ironically highlights Ihimaera's awareness of the true value of the rural world of the Maori. This value is best recognized, in other words, when it is under threat. In fact – again, ironically – the threat is that it is under-valued. This is a theme which Ihimaera develops in his later writings but which, nonetheless, is equally pronounced in *Pounamu, Pounamu*.

In both "The Child" and "The Whale", Ihimaera dramatises with a telling poignancy the fate of the old folks caught in a world that is divorced from anything they were brought up to believe in. Through recreating the world of Heta's Nanny Violet in the child's mind, Ihimaera attempts to make the past live in the present. For, as Heta tells his school friends who think that his Nanny is porangi: "No! I've seen what she looks at ... I've seen her world. She's taken me there" ("The Child," *Pounamu, Pounamu*, p. 108).

This theme is emphasised in "The Whale", but what pervades this story and raises the kaumatua's passing to the level of symbolism is a portentous sense of the demise of the world of the Maori, of Maori ways. Ihimaera writes that: "In this whanau, this old one is the last of his generation" ("The Whale," *Pounamu, Pounamu*, p. 115). Corballis and Garrett remark that "as the story proceeds we see that 'generation' signifies more than just age; the old man is the last living embodiment of the traditional Maori ways — of the 'happiness and aroha', the thriving whanau, the concern for Maoritanga and the Maori language itself."[10]

Ihimaera captures the kaumatua's heart-rending grief as he notes "the houses [which] are clustered close together, but [which are] closed to one another", symbolising the lack of aroha and of the spirit of whanaungatanga for one another:

> More visitors had arrived. They had come from the Whangarei, and they were tired and hungry. He saw their faces in the light. But people of his whanau, they were quarrelling with the visitors. They would not open the door to the storeroom. It was locked now. There would be no kai for the visitors. They had come too late. Heart was locking out heart. He was stunned, this old one. Always there was food, always aroha, always open heart. That was the Maori way. aroha.
>
> ... Bring me the axe .... The axe in his hand. He lifted it and ...
>
> —Aue ... The first blow upon the locked door. (*Pounamu, Pounamu*, pp. 120–1)

Ihimaera even at this stage of his development as a writer was painfully aware of the loss of the old values. He shows this through the old man's lament in "The Whale":

> Ae, even in his own day, Maoritanga had been dying. But not the spirit, not the joy of aroha .... The respect for Maori customs and Maori tapu, that too was disappearing .... The Maori of this time is different from the Maori of his own time. (*Pounamu, Pounamu*, pp. 118–9)

It was such "unMaori-like" attitudes as denying visitors traditional welcome and refreshments, coupled with the fact that attempts by elders to inculcate an appreciation of Maori cultural values in the new generation often meet with resistance, because the new generation could not reconcile the paradoxes inherent in both cultures of which they were hybrid products: this is what broke the kaumatua's heart:

> He'd told her that when she was a little girl. Even then the world had been changing. Hera, she'd been one of the few of his mokopuna who'd been interested in the Maori of the past. The rest, they'd felt the pull of the Pakeha world, like fish too eager to grab at a dangling hook. Only in Hera had he seen the spark, the hope that she might retain her Maoritanga. And he had taught her all he knew .... even Hera had changed as she grew older. She too, like many of the other young people, had gone away to the city. And when she had returned for a visit, this old one could see that the Pakeha life had proved too strong for her. He had tried to lead her back to his world, and she had quarrelled with him.
>
> —Don't, Nanny! The world isn't Maori any more. But it's the world I have to live in. You dream too much. Your world is gone. I can't live it for you. Can't you see? (*Pounamu, Pounamu*, pp. 116–7)

It was such regressions as Hera's, the lack of spirit of oneness and aroha, and particularly the fact that the old man was powerless to stop "the tide" of change, that finally destroyed the kaumatua's illusions. It is a rhetorical question that he intones at the end: "Where lies the blame ..." (p. 122).

In "The Other Side of the Fence" Ihimaera confronts some of the tensions of a multi-racial urban existence. He also contrasts the assumptions and perceptions inherent in both cultures and explores the dilemma of the new generation of Maori. Through the analysis of the Heremaia children, Ihimaera looks at some of the fundamental cultural differences in perception:

> But these were only incidental flaws, and all the Heremaia children possessed them. Jack Simmons could tolerate them, but there were two traits he would not stand: the curiosity in the Heremaia children which led them to 'borrowing'

> and then the audacity to deny that they were responsible .... Jack Simmons had since come to understand that borrowing was a common Maori trait: what's yours is mine, what's mine is yours. Maybe it was acceptable practice among Maori people but this city suburb was certainly not a Maori community. (*Pounamu, Pounamu*, pp. 44–5)

Ihimaera is implying that Maori and Pakeha have some adjustments to make if they have to live as next door neighbours: if Maori want to move to urban areas with dominant Pakeha residency, they have to recognise that a different code of values operates there—a Pakeha scale of values—which they would be expected to observe. If they, however, want to practice the Maori cultural and traditional values, they have either to do that in Maori communities where they would be understood and appreciated, or make allowances for Pakeha ignorance and misunderstanding.

The cultural difference is also exemplified by the Heremaia children's utter disregard for the fence that separates their property from the Simmons's:

> Jack Simmons watches as she runs across the back yard and climbs the fence between the two properties. He erected that fence three years ago. Come to think of it, the Heremaia children had helped him build it .... Jack Simmons smiles to himself. The fence might as well not exist. (*Pounamu, Pounamu*, p. 46)

By introducing the Maori dictum of "we share and share alike, ay," (p. 46) Ihimaera shows that the two families are operating according to different cultural codes and values. While the Simmonses are bent on maintaining their individualism and separateness, the Heremaias are exhibiting the openness of attitude which, Ihimaera believes, characterises Maori. Jack Simmons admits that "their humour may not always be in the best taste, but it is honest and open. And to hear them laugh is to hear laughter as it should be: punched straight from the chest with no holds barred" (p. 51). He also makes another admission:

> There were other characteristics in the Heremaia family which redeemed them totally. The greatest of these was their generosity. When the Simmonses had first settled in their new house they had had no furniture or cooking utensils because their household effects were still in transit from the landing port of Wellington. Sam and Millie had come to the rescue, and Millie had taken great delight in providing Maori bread along with the cutlery. Later, when the furniture arrived, Sam came around every day to help Jack Simmons move it into the house .... And it had been Millie apparently, who'd told Sam to get out the scythe and cut the Simmons's long grass when they were away on holiday one Christmas. (*Pounamu, Pounamu*, p. 53)

The observation that the Heremaias "stick out like a sore thumb in the neighbourhood" (p. 58) and that Maori "have not yet learnt the art of living with European people who may not understand their ways nor like them" enlarges upon the earlier comment made by Jack Simmons that "times had changed" and "the sooner they understood that, the better" (p. 46). In this context, Ihimaera recognizes that Maori should be aware of their Maoritanga, while at the same time acknowledging the need for them to accommodate Pakeha values. Being aware of their Maoritanga includes a level-headed appraisal of its strengths — family aroha, *whanaungatanga* (kinship and family responsibility), *manaakitanga* (reciprocal assistance to one another), and the priority given to the elders as custodians of traditional and cultural values. Interestingly, Ihimaera allows Jack Simmons an appreciation of these positive qualities (see above) as well as a judgement of the culture's negative aspects:

> The quicker Maori adjusted to European life the better. It was no use their trying to live in their

> old careless manner. They had to have some regard for their neighbours, accustomed to a more private mode of living. An Englishman's home was his castle; he preferred it that way. (*Pounamu, Pounamu*, p. 52)

The above remarks highlight fundamental differences originating from dissimilar cultural perspectives; they indicate Ihimaera's awareness of the erroneous but near-universal belief that the solution to the Maori's problems in a post-colonial society lies in assimilation.

Ihimaera believes that the key to the future for young Maori lies in their knowledge and adequate appreciation of their past, and an integration of this past with the present. Chinua Achebe, the Nigerian writer, puts it most succinctly with an Ibo proverb: "that a man who can't tell where the rain began to beat him cannot know where he dried his body".[11] Applied to a Maori context, this means that, for Maori to be truly biculturally integrated, they have first to come to terms with their Maoritanga, and then to reconcile it with Pakeha values.

Ihimaera's concern with the positive affirmation of Maoritanga is mirrored in the course of *Pounamu, Pounamu*, of which Richard Corballis has made an (as he says) "over-simplified" summary.[12] He notes a "movement from hope and laughter to despair and tears ... in the volume as a whole":

> ... at the front are the happier stories in which Maori values are affirmed positively ... at the back are the darker ones, in which these values are expressed in a negative way, through disillusionment, deprivation and death. In between lies a set of rather ambivalent stories: "Fire on Greenstone", in which a disastrous fire interrupts a loving affirmation of the spirit of the whanau; "The Other Side of the Fence", which depicts an uneasy truce between Maori and Pakeha values; and "In Search of the Emerald City" in which

> the child-narrator (Matiu) is left poised between town and country.[13]

What is striking in Corballis's summary is the appreciation of Ihimaera's hesitant exploration of the concept of biculturalism in "The Other Side of the Fence" and "In Search of the Emerald City". Concerned as Ihimaera was with depicting the virtues of Maori rural life in *Pounamu, Pounamu*, and with breaking the literary barriers mentioned earlier, he nevertheless realised that the most practical solution to the tensions in a post-colonial society is an adjustment of the demands of both Maori and Pakeha to suit the new social structure.

The world of Ihimaera's "Tangi" encapsulates one particular dimension of Maori culture—the emotional aspect. By projection, it also reflects the whole complex issue of traditional values, and Tama's attempt to come to terms with those values while still retaining his foothold in the Pakeha world. Tama's father, before he died, had passed on the mantle of responsibility to Tama, saying:

> *You must always look after your younger sisters and brothers, Tama. Your mother too, if I should die. Remember, Tama, always.*
>
> *Yes, Daddy.*
>
> *You are the eldest. That is your duty, your obligation. I was taught that as a child. I teach you that now.* (*Pounamu, Pounamu*, p. 129)

These are words which complement the (unspoken) teachings of Tama's Pakeha heritage, and which he intones as he tries to come to grips with his grief. Ihimaera has consistently upheld that his intention is to expound the "Maori landscape of the heart" as a complement to what John Beston has described as "emotional suppression in the white culture of New Zealand."[14] Ihimaera sees Maori people's emotional effusiveness—of grief as much as joy—as a celebration of Maori culture. He has told John Beston:

> I looked for the one major physical institution that Maori people retain in the most positive

> way and found it in the tangi, our ceremonial of mourning ... virtually the only institution we have for conveying our feelings about being Maori.[15]

Ihimaera's "Tangi" deals with themes which are developed in the novel, *Tangi*. Paul Katene remarks that: "*Tangi* is not only a personalised vision of the author, it is the personalised experience of a people—it is the heartbeat of Maoridom, told with great subtlety and sensitivity within a framework that remains peculiarly Maori."[16]

Tangi represents a synthesis of Maoritanga, and reflects Ihimaera's belief in Maori traditional values—of family commitment, collective participation, and the communal nature of Maori ceremonials such as the *tangihanga* itself. The traditional event becomes a vehicle, for Ihimaera, for examining his people's cultural values in a changing world.

Two aspects of *Tangi* are worthy of our special attention: the significance of the tangi to the concept of Maoritanga, and Tama's initial attempts at biculturalism.

Corballis and Garrett, in discussing the structure and narrative levels of *Tangi*, have noted that the novel relates three stories: "Firstly, there is a detailed account of Tama's changing reaction to his father's death .... Then there is the history of Tama's family and of his own upbringing. Thirdly, there is the legendary history of the Maori." The second and third levels of these stories afford Ihimaera the scope to expatiate on the concept of Maoritanga from different perspectives.

Through documenting Tama's family life and upbringing, as Corballis and Garrett observe, he tells "the story of one representative Maori family making its way in a world more and more dominated by the materialistic values of the Pakeha, but nevertheless a world in which an awareness of an older, indigenous culture still exists."

By adopting a typically Maori response, "the wholehearted abandonment" to the tangi as opposed to "the awkward reserve of the Pakeha," they say, Ihimaera highlights and enlivens its traditional basis.[17]

Drawn between two worlds, Maori and Pakeha, Tama needs the ceremonial progression of the tangi to reconcile himself to all the values of his Maori culture. His initial response when he heard the news of his father's death on the phone, and despite the restraint which his Pakeha environment demands, was to cry—although he cautions himself: "There is no time for tears" (*Tangi*, p. 19). But later, in a traditional environment he abandons himself to the grief: "Now that he is gone, they weep. Don't brush your own tears away. There is no shame in weeping. Let them fall, let them fall" (*Tangi*, p. 136). By the end of the tangi, Tama's Maoritanga has asserted itself through his having to perform the rites and calls associated with the tangi; with that, Tama not only conquers the initial emotional crisis, he is, as Corballis and Garrett acknowledge, "ready for the responsibilities of manhood" and of the leadership of the tribal family as the eldest son.

Ihimaera's use of Maori mythology, both in the thematic structure of *Tangi* and to carry the narrative, is also an affirmation of Maoritanga. In using Maori myths, Ihimaera claims (as already mentioned) that he is trying "to make the past live in the present." But essentially, the mythological background becomes a vehicle through which Tama conquers his grief, as with each remembered myth narrative he re-lives a memorable and happy occasion with a well-loved father:

> And I remember one magical afternoon when we were walking along Wainui Beach . . . .Dad knelt beside me, pointed toward the floats, and whispered a dream to me.
>
> —Look, Tama! See the Fleet coming? . . . . I followed his gaze and the floats indeed became the seven legendary canoes which brought the Maori to Aotearoa. (*Tangi*, p. 48)

Tama can cope with the overwhelming sense of panic at "the toppling over the abyss of his world", occasioned by his father's death, only through these "recalls".[18] The narrative technique flits forward and backward in time, capturing each moment in the immediate past at which Tama's father had played a prominent part in his life; and expressing the calm and comfort which a father figure gives to the intimidating world of a child:

> Do you remember, e pa, that time when you took me into town one crowded night so many years ago? I was only a little boy then, about five, I suppose. You wait here, you said .... I waited and waited, e pa. I was frightened. All those people, they jostled and pushed against me. They couldn't see me; I was so small. I felt as if I was in a land full of giants. In the end I cried, Dad. I couldn't help it ... and decided I would find you. (*Tangi*, p. 12)

By recollecting the calm which attended his world, through his father's resolution of such incidents and fears, and by linking his parents with the Maori creation myth, Tama attempts to stabilise himself, and contain his grief:

> His calm was his greatest possession .... My father was the Sky. He held dominion over night and day. He was both sun and moon, keeping constant watch over his children .... Now the Sky has fallen. (*Tangi, p. 52*)

Corballis and Garrett see Ihimaera's use of "the myth of the discovery of New Zealand" as being "intimately associated with the idea of being Maori .... Rongo Mahana repeats their names to his son .... 'They are the Maori, Tama. *As long as you remember them you are a Maori.*' "[19] They also see Ihimaera as functioning as "the traditional artist whose task is to resuscitate the myths that bind his culture together"; this task is most effectively summarised in their comment that:

> The story of Tama's personal discovery of his place in Maori society becomes a story of the reintegration of all the elements that constitute

> that society. The individual is incorporated into the family, the family into the tribal unit. This in turn is based upon, and given status by, the communal ownership and nurturing of the tribal land; and finally the whole social system and its attendant values are given meaning within the framework of a specific system of myths. These are some of the elements that constitute the idea of Maoritanga.[20]

Tama's initial attempts to reconcile the two cultural traditions, Maori and Pakeha, of which he is a product, is particularly significant to Ihimaera's concept of biculturalism. Having partly mastered his grief at the passing of his father, Tama embarks on his journey to confront his other heritage, his Pakeha side. But he bears the traditional Maori values on this journey. The tangi, its rites and rituals, and the remembrances during this harrowing period of his father's teachings and efforts to inculcate the traditional values in him, all arm Tama with enough knowledge for this future. Tama assures his dead father: "E pa, I remember" (*Tangi*, p. 22). But he is also aware that he cannot put the clock back, and must stride forward into a future that is dominated by Pakeha values: "The clock ticks, the clock ticks. Here I am on the railway platform, waiting for a train. I cannot stop the clock. You have left me, father" (*Tangi*, p. 13).

While Ihimaera explores the concept of biculturalism and shows the functioning of Maoritanga through the tangi, he also notes the problems associated with a multi-racial society. He sees the problems of racial discrimination, isolation, ignorance of the complexities and "otherness" of the other culture, and the handicap of competing with more adequately groomed Pakeha children at school, as something that all Maori children in similar circumstance have to take in their stride as part of their general experience: "They were a part of growing up" (*Tangi*, p. 77). Tama's puzzlement at the spite in the voice of the little girl as she calls him "—Maori boy! Maori boy!" and meeting the racially discriminating mother of his friend who refuses to allow him at her son's birthday party because he is Maori, are all part of a growing-up experience which, Ihimaera believes, Maori children should not allow to destroy either their aspirations or their future:

> I made friends with a boy who'd come from England and he asked me to come to his tenth birthday. Then his mother rang up and said he was sick so I couldn't come. I'd already bought him a present.
>
> —You take it round to his place, Mum said. You take some books for him too.
>
> So I went to see him. I knocked on the door. His mother answered it. Behind her, I could see my friend and other kids, dressed in party hats and playing. He saw me and was embarrassed.
>
> ... —Do you want to come in? his mother asked me hesitantly.
>
> —No thank you, I answered, trying to be brave. I gave my friend his present .... All this time, I could hear those other children laughing .... Then I went away, and I couldn't help it, the tears just came. I couldn't understand. (*Tangi*, p. 77)

Ihimaera also believes, however, that it is experiences such as this that encourage Maori children to drop out from school with the false notion that by working and being independent they are automatically shielded from further such humiliations. Mere chose to drop down from the top form to a lower class because, as she says: "There's no other Maori in that class. I didn't want to stay" (*Tangi*, p. 78). Tama reports that "school became more lonely as I progressed upwards from one form to the next. My Maori mates dropped out earlier and went out working" (p. 78). He claims that "I stayed at school because that was what Dad wanted." But as he grew older and tenaciously stayed on he realised that: "By then, it seemed as if the world had indeed changed. Or perhaps it's only as a child or young boy that you are hurt. I was never hurt again because I took a firm step forward into the Pakeha world." By taking the "firm step forward into the Pakeha world" Tama also "managed to stride both worlds" (*Tangi*, p. 78).

To Ihimaera, achieving this feat is difficult and, as in Tama's case, requires firmness, tenacity of purpose, and parental encouragement. Says Tama: "With some amusement, I recall it was difficult at first" (*Tangi*, p. 78). Yet, no matter how difficult bestriding both worlds is, Ihimaera's message seems to be that "the world [that Maori children are] growing up in [is] a Pakeha one" and they have to make the effort to fit into that world and also retain their Maoritanga. Tama recollects that because he was growing up in a Pakeha world, "it was difficult to retain my Maoritanga .... Sometimes, I even forgot my Maoritanga and its values" (*Tangi*, p. 78). In Ihimaera's view, the actions of some Maori parents and elders inadvertently encouraged this loss. Tama shows this as he questions why his uncle and his wife should prefer to sleep "on a mattress on the floor ... in the sitting room" and allow him, a younger person, to sleep on their double bed, contrary to Maori custom (p. 79).

Ihimaera concedes that bestriding both worlds could be difficult because there is always a tendency to conveniently forget the Maori part of one's heritage, especially on the part of the younger generation who view its obligatory demands as cumbersome:

> It was more difficult to live in two worlds as I grew older. The Maori part was so easy to forget. Not being Maori, but what being Maori meant; the customs, the traditions, Maori aroha. (*Tangi*, p. 79)

Tama needed constant reminders: "After a while I discovered that all I needed to do was to remember Dad and my whanau, my big Maori family, and my world would right itself" (p. 79). Ihimaera has always believed that, even though much of what constitutes Maoritanga is being eroded by the demands of an individualistic social structure, a vital component—"Maori aroha, the love we hold for one another"—still survives and will never die (p. 79). Tama's remark that "even when I was a boy ... [Maoritanga] was dying" (*Tangi*, p. 79) echoes the words of the kaumatua in "The Whale",[21] but he pledges to pass on the traditions:

> I will teach Hone and Marama of Maori aroha, the love we hold for one another, so that they will never be alone if some day they leave Waituhi and go to the city. I will teach them open heart and open life ... and the humour to laugh if the values of the Pakeha are too strong for them. (*Tangi*, pp. 79–80)

So in *Tangi*, through Tama, Ihimaera begins a sustained advocacy for biculturalism which is carried over into his second novel, *Whanau*.

The Transitional Phase

Whanau marks a new phase in Ihimaera's writing: of an intensified awareness of the reality of the disintegrating effects of urban migration on Maori consciousness. As Tama remarks in *Tangi*, "going to Wellington or any big city is the dream of most young people who live in a small country settlement far from anywhere" (*Tangi*, p. 158). What started, in *Pounamu, Pounamu* and *Tangi*, as a gentle probe of the disenchantment of the younger generation with rural living, in view of the attraction that urban centres hold for them, becomes a poignant, almost swan-song lament in *Whanau* for the world that was. While in *Pounamu, Pounamu* and *Tangi*, Ihimaera celebrates the affinity of the main characters with the land, Waituhi, and with Maoritanga, his stance in *Whanau* is more explicitly didactic. Tama and his parents saw coming back to Waituhi as a kind of home-coming:

> All our lives our family had lived so much a gypsy life that we held fast to Waituhi. For us, Waituhi wasn't just a few houses strung along a country road; it was our home and we had finally come home to stay. Unlike my friends who dreamed of leaving, I didn't care that the work was hard .... It didn't matter to me for Waituhi was my home. (*Tangi*, p. 158)

Despite the monotony of rural existence which was driving other young men away, Tama avows his sense of comfort and calm:

> for me, there was always a sense of contentment in feeling a rhythm beneath my feet. The heart-beat of the land. That season would follow season and that the rhythm would never alter. Knowing this brought me peace like no other I had known. (*Tangi*, p. 158)

Yet, in spite of his professed love of the land and his family, Tama left Waituhi for Wellington, because like most young people of his generation he felt "a certain restlessness" — the pull of the city was too strong for him to resist. As he claims: "The bright lights of Wellington attracted me" (*Tangi*, p. 159). In *Whanau*, Ihimaera sees this migration as only one of the many threats to both the spirit of Maoritanga and his concept of biculturalism for Maori, based as it is on the necessity of securing and maintaining one's Maori identity.

In *Pounamu, Pounamu*, *Tangi*, and *Whanau*, Waituhi is presented as a sanctuary from which some of the characters can escape the vicissitudes of life, their failure to make it in the more competitive Pakeha world, and social changes exemplified by the materialism and individualism that many feel are the hallmarks of the Pakeha-dominated society. Characters such as Mattie Jones, Sam Walker and Jack Ropiho, although they cling to this hope that Waituhi might serve as a sanctuary, also realise that it has become a kind of prison from which they cannot hope to escape because they have already failed in the Pakeha world.

Ihimaera shows the decline in attraction of the old communal and traditional ways of life for the younger generation of Maori as constituting a real threat to the existence of the whanau and the sustenance of the spirit of Maoritanga. Brian Murton has illustrated this decline of the attraction of the old ways for young Maori in his analysis of Waituhi. He notes the ambivalence in people's attachment to places, commenting that it "is not entirely a pleasurable experience":

> The places to which they are most committed may be the very centres of their lives, but they may also be oppressive and imprisoning. There is a sheer drudgery of place, a sense of being tied inexorably to *the* place, of being bound by the established scenes and symbols and routines.[22]

But Murton also believes that this "drudgery is a part of profound commitment to a place, and any commitment must involve an acceptance of the restrictions that that place imposes. Our experience of place, especially of home, is a dialectical one—balancing a need to stay with a desire to escape".[23] This ambivalence of his characters concerning Waituhi occurs in much of Ihimaera's writing. As already indicated, it is expressed succinctly by Tama Mahana in *Tangi*, who left Waituhi "for Wellington after he saw his friends going: he was content yet discontent, happy yet unhappy."[24]

Corballis notes that *Whanau* "is a celebration of the spirit of whanau (family)."[25] But it is a celebration tinged with regret at the change that is taking place in Maori communities and villages, at the disillusionment of more and more Maori children with the rural way of life, and at the intensified urban drift occasioned by landlessness and the attraction of the bright lights of the city.

The opening chapters of *Whanau* introduce both the camaraderie which only the closeness of a village atmosphere can foster in people as diverse as those Ihimaera assembles in Charlie Whatu's truck; and also the disillusionment of some of the villagers with rural existence:

> People of the village of Waituhi huddle together on the tray. They are past caring about their neat clothes, the clothes they put on for special occasions .... Hine leans back against the side of the tray. She is blissfully tired. For one day she has been happy, one solitary day among all those stretching backward and in front of her. But not to worry about the grey days ahead ... (*Whanau*, pp. 2–3)

In spite of his introductory remark depicting Waituhi as "a back-water place," the warmth Ihimaera feels for the village is apparent. He sees the family, both nuclear and extended, as the most important vehicle in the propagation of a culture as orally based as Maori culture is. Ihimaera, however, also sees the family as the first casualty of both the new wave of individualism which Maori children are embracing, and of the deprivation of the "stress-absorbing" system of *manaakitanga* in the urban environment. Ihimaera uses family, particularly the Maori word *whanau*, symbolically to represent Maoridom in microcosm. Nelson Wattie says that the full meaning of the word *whanau* "can scarcely be conveyed in English, except perhaps by writing the novel [*Whanau*] which Ihimaera has done", and that *Whanau* "from one point of view ... is the definition of a word."[26]

Ihimaera thus equates the disintegration of many Maori families that he sees taking place in the face of the harsh realities of an urban environment with what has been happening to a larger Maoridom. The family disintegrations have far-reaching consequences for Ihimaera's concept of biculturalism, and a brief analysis of the traditional Maori family structure will show how its collapse contributes to the post-colonial tensions depicted in Ihimaera's fiction.

The Maori notion of family differs radically from the Pakeha concept in many ways. Although the extended family system is practised by both Maori and Pakeha in differing guises, the Pakeha society's emphasis on individualism makes the nuclear family the focus. Conversely, the Maori family is all-encompassing. The clan in a traditional society is the first level of the family. The clan in this context will be defined as an "extended family unit", who in all probability bear the same surname by virtue of descent; women often change their surnames when they marry, but they and their children retain by descent their kinship and affiliation to the maternal clan. This clan is still wider than what Ihimaera calls a sub tribe:

> the effective unit was the sub tribe with strong local ties, very definite boundaries and membership demarcated by a combination of descent from a local ancestor and residence ... the sub tribe were further divided into extended family units or kinship groups, closely related by blood and centred on a village gathering place. (*Maori*, p. 10)

Essentially the extended family unit would have one person as the head of "the family". Traditionally this position is hereditary and is occupied by the eldest son of the eldest son *ad infinitum*. Rongo before he dies tells Tama in *Tangi*: "You just remember, Tama. You're the eldest. Look after your mother and the family. Okay?" (*Tangi*, p. 22) Tamatea in *The Matriarch* echoes this, saying: "I was the eldest son of an eldest son, and the mantle of responsibility for the tribal family was mine whether I wanted it or not" (*The Matriarch*, p. 53). Ihimaera writes that although "the active leadership of [the family] was generally a male prerogative", where the eldest son at any point does not have a son, at his death, leadership of the family could still be retained by the eldest daughter:

> sometimes, however, it happened that the first-born of the senior rangatira line was not a male but rather a woman. She was then made a priestess and accorded the greatest respect as a wahine ariki. (*The Matriarch*, pp. 207–8)

The essential function of this headship, as in Ibo society, would be to ensure that "an elder does not watch a nanny goat give birth on tether".[27] This implies that elders have a duty to perpetuate the culture through teaching the younger generation what to do. As Ihimaera says: "The eldest always look after the younger ones of the family. Not only his own family, but *all* the family" (*Whanau*, p. 112).

The traditional family, as Ihimaera has described it, is structured on the basis of loyalty to the family and the tribe:

> ... the tribal identity rather than individual identity is expressed. It is an emotional identity based on the concept of aroha or love and sympathy for one another as members of a family, and whanaungatanga which stresses the obligatory links of duty and aid for each other. (*Maori*, p. 11)

This concept is echoed by David Cook in his study of African literature:

> In traditional society, the individual is seen first and foremost as part of a corporate whole, and his existence as part of the social pattern overwhelms any private life he might lead within the confines of his own consciousness. Such a life is relatively public: it is not easy to keep secrets nor is it thought desirable to do so. In such a situation, social conventions exert great authority. The communal good is all-important and any personal denial of group commitment appears to weaken the whole and is deplored. Contribution to the life and welfare of the community is the greatest good, and hence individualism is seen as negative.[28]

This type of family structure and tradition does not only emphasise these obligations in principle; but the existence and continued sustenance of the whanau depends on the contributions of all individuals in the family to it. In turn the individual is dependent on the family for economic and social well-being, since farming, fishing and hunting are communal activities, as well as occasions like marriages and deaths, including burial ceremonies. During farming periods, for example, the whole family (comprising all the nuclear families) would gather, plough the family lands and cultivate them:

> Until last year, the Mahana clan would get together at a family meeting, dub in some money and buy seed to plant in the family paddocks. Then they would fix a time for the planting, calculating it the old way by the shape of the moon and the position of the stars in the night sky. Once that was done, they would all come together at the planting. It used to be a good time. A family occasion. A gathering of the Mahana clan. Kids and all would come to follow the tractor and plant the seeds in the furrows. And although it was hard work it didn't seem to take long because everybody was too busy chucking off at each other to think of how hard the work was. (*Whanau*, p. 50)

When the farm crops are harvested, each nuclear family gets an equitable share corresponding to its need and size: "once the crop was ready, the Mahana clan would come together again. They would gather the harvest and there would be fulfillment of family reaping a shared labour" (*Whanau*, p. 51). Ihimaera thus sees these interdependencies as forces of cohesion, binding the members of the whanau firmly together. He also believes that the growing emphasis on individuality in the post-colonial era has eroded these cohesive forces, creating tensions. Whereas in the pre-European era, it was a community spirit that was applauded, the post-Pakeha social structure emphasises self-dependency:

> There is security in having and keeping one job, in having permanent employment. And living in the cities is nothing but an attractive trap. It binds you to itself with contracts: with high mortgages or steep rents, with hire purchase

> payments and threats of repossession. And it asks more of you: more of your money and more and more for things you did not really want. A venus flytrap. And once you're caught, you can never escape. You must keep working and keep working to keep up the next payment. You can't afford to take a week or two off for something as ridiculous as the family planting. (*Whanau*, p. 53)

Even more important than the economic function of the family structure are the social and cultural functions. The society, as Ihimaera points out, regulates the behaviour of its members and has checks and balances to ensure their adherence to societal norms and also to curb excesses. This is particularly effective in traditional rural areas where everyone knows everyone else. These mechanisms of censure are most effective because the young are socialised from birth to be conscious of their cultural and social obligations and to perform those duties that enhance the common good of the community. One of the mechanisms which the society utilises is the closeness of individuals in a family. Ihimaera sees the family bond as very important in Maori relationships and, even without the almost suffocating love that Tama exhibits for his father in *Tangi* as an example, the effect, or lack of it, of this bond pervades Ihimaera's writing.

In *Whanau*, despite the kaleidoscope of characters, the children playing outside the houses are recognised and acknowledged by each passing individual and the whanau. What is important, in Ihimaera's view, is that through these acknowledgements we become aware that the society is ever watching after these children. Nothing they do—their games, pranks, fights—passes unnoticed. For example, Pene and his Nanny Paora notice the kite that the children are flying, making Pene recall the story of Tupurupuru; while Andrew Whatu, cleaning Rongopai with his father, also notices the same kite:[29] "He looks up and sees the painted eaves of Rongopai holding up the sky. High above it a kite is dancing in the wayward current" (*Whanau*, p. 124). And Miro Mananui yells at the children to "take [their] fullas football somewhere else ... watches with eagle eyes to make sure those kids shut the gate after them" (*Whanau*, p. 102).

The closeness of members of both the nuclear family and the extended family coupled with the spirit of manaakitanga makes anyone's business everyone's business. This ensures the conformity of the individual with the traditional norms and fosters cultural continuity, although to the younger generation, this "noseyness" is restrictive and claustrophobic. Hence, away from these cultural restrictions, the young experience a kind of liberation which, together with the Pakeha emphasis on individualism, make some of these children reckless. To Ihimaera, there is a contrast between the children raised on traditional rural Maori hearths and their counterparts in urban environments. While in the rural environment it is the duty of parents and the society—represented by the extended family—to mould the characters of the young, in an urban environment this is left to parents and, to some extent, teachers, alone.

These affirmations of communal values and the inherent advantages of rural existence are not shared by many of the younger generation. Yet Ihimaera's feeling for Waituhi is such that it gives rise to authorial intrusion, noted by Michael King, which is most effusive when Ihimaera describes the aroha and communal spirit that suffuses the village.[30] His feelings are clear, for instance, in the way he describes the kind of reception a stranger to Waituhi would receive from one of the whanau:

> He may ask you: Have you relations in the village? And if you've none, he'll say: Well, where will you stay? .... Then he'll probably tell you you'd better stay at his place for the night and catch the bus back to the city with him in the morning .... You'll remember them with affection. (*Whanau*, pp. 7–9)

Excluding the whanau itself, which is the central character in *Whanau*, Ihimaera creates four distinct types of characters and uses their feelings and affinity for the whanau and for Waituhi as reference points in assessing the degree of their biculturalism. This barometric pointer is able to be used in reference to the wider concept of biculturalism because Waituhi is representative of a wider Maoridom. As already mentioned, Ihimaera sees a truly bicultural Maori as anyone who could effectively integrate his or her dual—Maori and Pakeha—heritages without feeling a stranger to either world.

Characters such as Sam Walker, Mattie Jones, and Jack Ropiho constitute the first group who fit neither into the Maori world, because they cannot reconcile themselves to its rigid demands and ethics, nor into the Pakeha world, having already failed in that system. Sam Walker had gone to jail for bashing a taxi driver over the head; Mattie Jones has an illegitimate child and is still to recover from the trauma of being jilted by George Karepa; Jack Ropiho could not hold down a job out of laziness and drunkenness, and eventually was driven back to Waituhi by near-starvation. Ihimaera does not believe that there is much to expect from these characters and sums them up as no-hopers:

> Good old Sam, who knew exactly what he was, a no-hoper, and *that nothing he could do would ever change that* .... Good old Sam with good old Mattie. Two of a kind, the bad kind. Both of them back here where they know they belong. Back here, *because there is nowhere else to go.* (*Whanau*, p. 57) [italics added]

It should be noted that, while these characters are not prepared to commit themselves to Maori society with its attendant obligations, they are nevertheless willing to benefit from that society's open-handed generosity.

Charlie Whatu, his wife, Rongo Mahana, Miro Mananui, and Nanny Paora belong to the group who fit only into the Maori world because that is where they feel most at home. They are so used to the Maori way of life that they feel alienated in a Pakeha world. This is the group which, Ihimaera says,

> will never leave because they and the village are inseparable. They have been too steeped in family life .... They give life to the village; the village gives life to them. Away from it they will wither. (*Whanau*, pp. 17–8)

Hana Walker and Sonny Whatu are typical examples of the third group — of the restless young generation who are disillusioned with rural existence and the old ways of life. For them, Waituhi is a "dump, a hick town, and a nothing place"; they believe that there is nothing in such a place for them. (*Whanau*, p. 14) Ihimaera says that, for this group, the desire to get away from the village is like a fever.

Ihimaera illustrates his concept of biculturalism for Maori through such characters as Hepa Walker, Pene Jackson, and Andrew Whatu. These are the ones who fit into both worlds without being strangers in either:

> [Hepa Walker], like his Pakeha friends, believed that the future for New Zealand lay in the integration of the two races Maori and Pakeha. One particular incident had convinced him of this. He had been invited to a lecture given by a Wellington economist at which that learned gentleman had illustrated with graphs, statistics and demographic projections that more movement of Maori from the lower classes into the middle class bracket was necessary to promote the quicker integration of the Maori into the European way of life. At first, sitting there, Hepa had felt both rage and embarrassment. But as the lecture had continued, he had found himself agreeing with the economist.
> (*Whanau*, pp. 35–6)

This economic theory, of an upward movement of Maori in the social and economic ladder promoting a faster rate of bicultural integration, is one with which Ihimaera generally agrees. His reservation, it must be said, is not with the concept, but with characters such as Hepa Walker who see the theory as having a one-dimensional application — that of enhancing their prestige. Ihimaera's initial definition of biculturalism for Maori included characters such as Hepa Walker, for at this stage Ihimaera's main concern was in fostering a desire to integrate the positive aspects of the Maori and Pakeha cultures; he believed, then as now, that it behoves all New Zealanders to create an environment in which both races can live together in peace. His subsequent portrayal of Hepa Walker as having a minimal understanding of what really constitutes biculturalism points to Ihimaera's awareness of the shortcomings of the concept (which will be treated later in this section).

Ihimaera, like Hepa Walker and other Maori elders, believes that educational achievement is a key factor in this upward movement, and consequently in the movement towards biculturalism for Maori. As Hepa reflects,

> When you thought about it, more middle-class Maori would solve many problems, many inconsistencies in the present situation. The crime rate would go down, wouldn't it? The social differences would be minimised, wouldn't they? The intangible and never-to-be admitted discrimination between Maori and Pakeha would disappear, surely? All this would happen, yes, when the Maori rose from lower to middle-class stature. (*Whanau*, p. 36)

Despite the irony, Ihimaera believes that this upward mobility has the potential for good, and sees characters such as Pene and Andrew Whatu as embodying this hope. Furthermore, Ihimaera demonstrates this belief not only through the pronouncements of characters such as Hepa Walker and Huia Mahana in *Whanau*, Mrs Heremaia in "Catching Up", and Teria Mahana in *The Matriarch*; he is himself a living example and symbol of it.

The Political Phase

The New Net Goes Fishing represents the beginning of Ihimaera's political development as a writer and as a spokesperson on contemporary issues of relevance to Maori.

Having realised the disintegrating effects of urban migration and the discontent of the younger generations with rural existence, Ihimaera in *The New Net Goes Fishing* analyses the break-up of the family unit and the loss of the community spirit and solidarity on which the culture had hitherto depended and by which it had always been sustained.

Themes that he had explored in such short stories as "In Search of the Emerald City" and "The Whale", among others in *Pounamu, Pounamu*, and that he developed in *Tangi* and *Whanau*, are once more highlighted. But in *The New Net Goes Fishing*, these themes are given an urgency which is illustrative of their contemporary importance.

Considering that, before the 1960s, oral literature was the means of cultural transmission and preservation, and that the urban centres could not adequately foster the traditional Maori cultural values, the inability of some Maori parents to perform this function of perpetuating the culture through teaching their children those values resulted in the development of what Ihimaera calls a cultural "faultline" (*The Matriarch*, p. 232).

Ihimaera believes that, unfortunately, some of these parents were themselves in dire need of guidance to adapt to Pakeha ways; many genuinely felt that Maori culture would be an impediment rather than an asset to their children and so refused to impart what they themselves knew of it to their children. Because of the new individualism which saw children doing whatever they felt like doing, with many rootlessly and aimlessly drifting without guidance, the elders could not impart the culture to them even if they wanted to, because the younger generation were not always around:

> How can the old generation teach the new generation if they are not there to listen? Ah yes, this is how the discontinuity developed between the old and the young. It was a great faultline, right across the population. (*The Matriarch*, p. 232)

Ihimaera's *The New Net Goes Fishing* presents an urban reality that is at variance with what obtains in rural Maori villages. "In Search of the Emerald City" shows, as Alistair Fox remarks, that "the land where dreams may come true turns out in fact, for some, to be the infernal city .... Through the eyes of two young children, we see how the old family unity and aroha can disintegrate under the pressures of urban society."[31] The dream to make it in the Pakeha world, like "the myth of the search for emerald city", is shattered by the realisation that the city, in Beston's words, "is not a generous world."[32]

The pavement of the emerald city, as Ihimaera says, could be hard on the soles of the feet. As these pressures mount, the traditional bonds of aroha, whanaungatanga, and manaakitanga all come under severe strain and, as in the case of "Big Brother, Little Sister", may break asunder. Parents have become individualistic, placing their own happiness or the pursuit of this happiness above their responsibility both to their family and to the larger society; the family bonds and aroha which Ihimaera sees as sustaining the whanau and the culture are gone.

Ihimaera gives varied reasons for the break-up of the families. One is the migration to urban areas occasioned by the lack of permanent jobs in the rural areas:

> —No more jobs back home, he told uncle. Plenty of the seasonal work, yes, but me and Hine had enough of that. We had enough of shearing, the fruit-picking and the going down south to shear some more. No, plenty of work in Wellington. Plenty of factories. (*The New Net Goes Fishing*, pp. 5–6)

Ihimaera sees the consequences of these migrations as, first, the splintering of the whanau as families such as Matiu's leave, and the loss of both the communal spirit and the solidarity which had been the corner-stone of life in the villages. In "Gathering of the Whakapapa" Ihimaera says that it is the love that Nanny Tama has for the village family that drove him on to reconstruct the whakapapa in spite of his failing health and old age:

> Slowly and gradually he had gathered the whakapapa. Painstakingly, he'd assembled it and checked it and added to it. His strength went into the whakapapa. His aroha for us drove him relentlessly to the task. (*The New Net Goes Fishing*, p. 30)

This aroha is reciprocated by the village, showing the community spirit that exists in the whanau:

> The village people should have been asleep but no, there they were, waiting for us. The tears flowed down Nanny Tama's face.
>
> —Huh? he asked Dad. What's wrong with you fullas! Loving hands reached out to him as we carried him through the assembly. Everywhere, voices welcomed him. (*The New Net Goes Fishing*, p. 36)

Arvidson, commenting on the naturalness of the traditional bonds, notes that in "Gathering of the Whakapapa", "we see the subtle strength of aroha as an ethical principle .... it is the only story in *The New Net Goes Fishing* which asserts unhesitatingly and without qualification both the fundamental sufficiency of Maoritanga and its ability to survive without deliberate conscious cultivation."[33]

In *Whanau*, Ihimaera mentions that in earlier times it was the communal spirit that sustained even large tournament hui:

> In the old days, the whole whanau would help out with the tournament. You didn't really need

> money to feed visiting people. Somebody donated a pig, somebody else a sheep .... The men took time off to put up the marquees. The women baked the bread .... People spare what they can, both time and money. It may not be much, but at least it's something. (*Whanau*, p. 85)

But he sees the modern social structure based on individual aims and aspirations as destroying this community spirit:

> People couldn't come for a week in the spring. If they came, they lost their jobs .... Can't blame them really. And can't blame people when they don't pitch in together to help out at the tournaments. Money is hard to come by these days. Time is hard to give, too. It's not that people around here are lazy; they're just too busy to help I suppose. (*Whanau*, p. 85)

The other reason for the loss of communal commitment, in Ihimaera's view, is the dream to make it in the Pakeha world, and the additional desire of parents to give their children a better life than they had. Most feel the "good life" can best be achieved in urban areas:

> We'll make lots of money and be rich as anything because Wellington is where the money is. And you have to go where the money is, ay Dad. No use staying in Waituhi and being poor all the time, ay .... I want us to have a good life, a new start, Dad tried to explain. A new start for my kids. Me and Hine, we've always had nothing. But my kids? They're going to grow up with everything. I'll fight for it, because they must have it. (*The New Net Goes Fishing*, pp. 3–6)

The conceptualisation of these dreams and their many facets is essential for an appreciation of the subsequent "reality-generated" tensions. These dreams are arbitrarily divided into three categories for ease of comprehension.

The first category, as mentioned above, is people's dreams to make good in the Pakeha world, which is closely related to the dream of parents for their children.

Ihimaera links urban migration with joblessness, as Matiu's father says earlier, and with land issues, saying: "the landlessness of the people combined with the power of the Pakeha coin to attract Maori to the cities in great numbers" (*The Matriarch*, p. 232). This attraction of "Pakeha coin" is considerable, and when combined with the scintillating tales of the fun to be had in the cities, often proves irresistible. Watene in "The House with Sugarbag Windows" is drawn by the dream of riches:

> He wanted what he'd never had. He visualised it in terms of a two-storey red brick house, money in the bank and two cars in the garage. Nothing was going to stop him from getting it. (*The New Net Goes Fishing*, p. 162)

Some of these dreams, as Hana Walker's in *Whanau*, are alluringly childish:

> She wants to have a good time *now*. All the other kids leave school early, so why can't she? Yes, and once she gets away from here, she'll buy lots of dresses and go to all the dances. She'll never go to bed; why sleep when there's so much to do? .... And she envies her older cousins when they come back to the village from Auckland or Wellington. They tell her of the fantastic time they're having. (*Whanau*, p. 14)

Hana Walker's naivety aside, her disillusionment with her environment and yearning for city life epitomise the predicament of many Maori children in post-colonial society. (This disillusionment is at variance with the experience of children in a pre-Pakeha traditional set-up, for reasons which have already been appraised.)

The dream of parents to make the lives of their children better than theirs is related both to the desire to make good in the Pakeha world and to the attraction of money. It is of course the dream of all good parents to make the lives of their offspring better, but the post-colonial problems of the Maori parents add a poignancy to this dream:

> The Rongo Mahana family live in the city, in a tidy wooden house in a tidy wooden suburb. They have lived there three years now. That Huia, that hoha wife of Rongo's, had suddenly decided it would be best for the kids. She's wanted them nearer to the schools, nearer to the library and away from the no-hopers of the village. She wasn't going to see *her* kids going to the pack and growing wild, not on your life! No, her kids were going to get the best—whatever that was—and be nearer to civilisation. You think she slaved all her life for nothing? Think she went out into the paddocks picking maize all day for fun? Well if you did, just you think again. She's done everything for her kids. Suffered for them. Fought for them. And she'll keep on fighting for them. Because she's known what its like to go to school in rags, to know nothing and have nothing, and to be laughed at for being so poor ... she's known it all, known it all. And she's making sure that her kids don't feel the pain and the hurt of being dirt. (*Whanau*, p. 48)

Most Maori parents, Ihimaera says, realised that with the changes wrought in their society by the coming of the European, with the limited farmlands available and even more limited capital to develop the land in tune with the modern concepts of farming, the only lasting legacy that they could leave their children was to equip them to fit into the "new ways" through education. Matiu, Christopher's father in "Return From Oz", who is also the young Matiu of "Yellow Brick Road", describes this dream and the attendant urban migration succinctly for his young son, Christopher:

> Waituhi .... Not as far as London or New York, but Dad told me that for him and for all Grandfather's family that journey they took so long ago was as great and important as any taken by people coming to New Zealand from overseas .... just as Mum's parents had come by ship from England in search of a new life, so had his parents come from Waituhi for the same reason. It didn't really matter ... that the distances were different because their dreams and hopes were just the same. (*The New Net Goes Fishing*, p. 193)

Matiu's father expatiates on this by saying that his wife had only come along to Wellington twenty years ago because she felt it was an obligation she owed her children to give them a better chance to fit into the "new world":

> You know, son, some times I wonder whether her heart was in our coming down here. She knew we had to come but I don't think she wanted to leave Waituhi. She was a brave woman, your mother. During all the years we lived here in Wellington she pretended to like it. But the truth is that she hated it .... We only came down here for him [Matiu] and your Auntie Roha. (*The New Net Goes Fishing*, p. 192)

To Christopher's pointed question as to the real reason they came to Wellington, his grandfather answers:

> Because I wanted the family to have the best of both worlds .... Twenty years we lived here, mokopuna. I steered my family down here, I suppose just like the navigators of the canoe which brought our people to Aotearoa long ago. Your Nanna didn't want to come but she knew we had to. There were no jobs back home. There didn't seem to be any future for our family if we stayed .... And we saw our children, your father and your Auntie Roha, do well in the world, and

> we were satisfied. We gave them the best we could. (*The New Net Goes Fishing*, pp. 195–6)

The second category of dreams is the nostalgia for the "old ways", the dream for a retention and preservation of whatever is left of traditional life. At its simplest level, it is an unadulterated appreciation, and contentment with the kind of communal existence which only a closely knit village can engender:

> She looks out at the village. All her life she has lived here. She has never known any other life except village life. Yet, her breath still catches at this sight of it, so bright and beautiful in the morning sun. Home. (*Whanau*, p. 6)

Mrs Charlie Whatu's joyful contentment, when contrasted with Sonny Whatu's disillusionment, is used to emphasise the rootlessness of the new generation, and the gulf between the young and the old:

> —Yeah, back to the sticks, Sonny Whatu growls moodily. Back to the nothing place, the nowhere place. Back to the boredom and a life which is a wash of grey without any bright colour. Back in Waituhi. Back in the middle of silence. (*Whanau*, p. 6)

The appreciation of the "old ways" which was a dominant theme in *Pounamu, Pounamu*, *Tangi*, and *Whanau* is echoed in such short stories as "Gathering of the Whakapapa" (already discussed), "The Greenstone Patu", and "Return from Oz". In the latter case, the reason given for Christopher's grandfather's journey back to Waituhi, according to the grandfather, is to draw his family there so that they "can get to know [their] Maori home" while he (the grandfather) is still living.

Included in the second category of dreamers are the middle-aged parents caught between two worlds: the old Maori ways in which they grew up, and the new Pakeha ways in which their children must find their individual places. As Christopher's grandfather tells him in "Return from Oz":

> Mokopuna, the Pakeha way is hard to fight and it is much easier to give in to it, to drift along with it. It was only when your Nanna died and was taken back to Waituhi that I saw how far the family had drifted apart from their people. No matter how often we'd returned to Waituhi I could see in their eyes the very thing I'd been blind to: that we were strangers to them at home. (*The New Net Goes Fishing*, p 196)

The predicaments and agonies of some of these parents are even more poignant because they know that some of the traditions they valued, while still useful to them, are useless to their children in the face of the new values. Yet they as parents, even while helplessly bewildered by these new values, have to help their children overcome their fear of the unknown. Some of them, even as they fight for their children, pushing and cajoling them to find their feet in the new Pakeha world, themselves crave the peace and tranquility that only the known, the familiar, the village can give:

> Yes, there was no doubt about it. Someday, maybe when the kids had found their own ways in the world, he and Huia would return. This is their home. This is their heart. (*Whanau*, p. 48)

The third category is the dream of bicultural integration. This, in Ihimaera's view, essentially involves an acceptance of the dual heritages, Maori and Pakeha, which he sees as the birth-right of all New Zealanders, and a coming to terms with the demands of both. It is the realisation of the distinction between assimilation and biculturalism—that acculturation is the attendant consequence of assimilation, while biculturalism implies a retention of both Maori and Pakeha cultures—which has shaped Ihimaera's modern perspective. He believes that there is a general misconception which equates biculturalism with assimilation; but that the distinction is vital. The old assumptions are, in any case, starting to be questioned in the popular media. Carroll Wall, for instance, writes that:

> The concept of assimilation that I was brought up with and which seemed such a fine idea at the time, has been flung aside by the Maori. They don't see themselves as being merely providers of a few dusky and musical genes to shore up the easily-sunburned and Calvinistic features of the white majority. What they want is their own racial identity, and they are going for it with a gusto.[34]

But the idea of biculturalism, in a post-colonial setting, is complex and difficult in its application. While many of the short stories in *The New Net Goes Fishing* explore the concept of biculturalism, with characters such as George in both "Clenched Fist" and "Tent on the Home Ground", Matiu in "Return from Oz",[35] and Rangi in "The Kids Downstairs" all exemplifying aspects of it, most of the stories, while confronting the doubts and unease about the concept highlighted in *Whanau* and the earlier "pastoral" writings, offer no easy answers.

"Big Brother, Little Sister" exposes the assaults on such concepts as family aroha, which are the result of parents striving for personal happiness and individualism without regard for the traditional concept of *whanaungatanga*. Ihimaera believes that in the new social structure, and away from the support of such traditional values and concepts as *manaakitanga*, some parents' failures to "make it" generate punitive attitudes within the nuclear family, with the children bearing the brunt of self-directed anger:

> Hema ran to the door and opened it. Dad had forced Mum against the wall and his hands were squeezing her throat.
>
> —Dad. Mum. Don't. Dad yelled at him and pushed him back into the bedroom.

> —Get back to bed, you damn kid .... Uncle Pera had taken off his belt. Just before he began to thrash Hema with it, he kicked the door closed.
>
> —Mum, Hema had called. The door was closing on her face. She did not come to stop this man. She did not come to her son. She did not .... The pain. He held his body tight against the blows. All he could think of was his mother, standing there, not helping him ....
>
> —Mum doesn't need us any more, he'd said. She doesn't need me ... (*The New Net Goes Fishing*, pp. 11–26)

Not only that; Ihimaera believes that such brutalized children will grow up assuming aggression is normal, developing attitudes such as those shown in "Passing Time". To these children, forming gangs and flitting in and out of jails become a way of life:

> She'd become accustomed to seeing the six kids together .... At the time the kids had seemed frightening. Menacing. Vibrating an aura of such hostility that people entering or leaving the concourse would by-pass them warily and isolate them in a distinct space which served only to make them appear more obvious, more ominous .... Even their silences caused tension, that was the strangest puzzle of all. It seemed they didn't need to do anything to cause it at all except just be there .... Behind the blackness, beneath the skin scored like the jackets with tattooed stars and strange dedications, underlying the hard eyes and arrogant lips, she had seen kids, who'd probably just left school. Bored. Wanting a bit of fun. The trouble was the world they lived in was no playground. Perhaps that was why two of the kids were missing today. (*The New Net Goes Fishing*, pp. 63–4)

Ihimaera's fiction captures the hopelessness of these children, as they bait the police while "passing time", waiting to be thrown into jail for the umpteenth time. The familiar cycle of expectation and consequence is the only thing they know:

> The kids laughed and their eyes sparkled with excitement.
>
> —Oh, we'll wait here until the other cops come .... When they arrive they'll hassle us and we'll hassle them. It's a kind of game, see. And maybe they'll take us for a ride, ay. We'll have a bit of fun. (*The New Net Goes Fishing*, p. 68)

In another instance of expecting the inevitable, one of the two nameless characters in "Truth of the Matter", narrating their misadventure to a cellmate, says of his associate: "But my mate didn't want any trouble .... Never been inside before. Shit, he has to learn. Soon be thinking of this place as home, yeah" (*The New Net Goes Fishing*, p 124).

But it is Ihimaera's development of the theme of biculturalism—and his unease with some aspects of it—that many of the stories are concerned with. All of his earlier writings have delved into this theme, *Pounamu, Pounamu* and *Tangi* only lightly, with *Whanau* revealing Ihimaera's ambivalence with the concept particularly because, as mentioned earlier, many equate it with assimilation. However, the Maori characters in Ihimaera's fiction reflect degrees of integration into society. The most developed characters are either those who have found their niche in the new world and literally bestride both worlds, or are contentedly entrenched in their Maoritanga.

An analysis of this category of the dreams makes it clear that some characters equate economic success, which is a realisation of their dream to make good in the Pakeha world, with being biculturally integrated. Hepa Walker in *Whanau*, for example, equates the outward show of affluence with bicultural integration:

> Hepa had taken a long and critical look at his own way of life. It was not that it was wanting anything; just that it could be improved by at least another car, a cocktail cabinet, a few pieces of crystal and a classical record collection. (*Whanau*, p. 36).

Also, he is happy with his son Frank's academic progress because it has made him proud and proved that the Maori was "as good as the Pakeha"— not because of his son's self-improvement (*Whanau*, p. 31).

Ihimaera is of the opinion that Hepa Walker does not realise that his material acquisitions do not constitute Pakeha values, for "they had given only a semblance of middle-class standards. Actually attaining the attitudes that went with them was much harder" (*Whanau*, p. 36). The author has reservations about Hepa Walker despite the latter's social and material successes:

> he has made it. A personnel officer in a local city firm, Hepa can socialise with the best of them. He plays golf on Saturdays, drinks in the best bars, attends the best church, and is on first-name terms with the district elite. In every way, he is a success. (*Whanau*, p. 36)

This reservation stems, in part, from Hepa Walker's attitude, and his inability to transcend the limitations of his background:

> He ... had not even been aware of the qualities, social and personal, which were required if ever he was to prove acceptable to Pakeha society. His progress had been marked by one social gaffe after another, but his saving grace had been an honesty which led his Pakeha friends to overlook his deficiencies with good humour. They had tolerated him, he was quite a fine chap really, and anyway they needed a Maori to sit with them at the opening ceremonies—of a new post

> office, new municipal building, new school—and to appear with them in the social pages of the local newspaper. (*Whanau*, p. 35)

Ihimaera's reservation also stems from Hepa Walker's limited perception of what bicultural integration really entails: that it is more of an attitude than a matter of material success. Ihimaera believes that economic and academic success, although they are keys to this integration, do not in themselves constitute integration, contrary to Hepa Walker's—and many others'—view.

It is the same limited vision that makes Watene, in "The House with Sugarbag Windows", perceive Pakeha values purely in material terms: "He visualised it in terms of a two-storey red brick house, money in the bank and two cars in the garage" (*The New Net Goes Fishing*, p. 162). To Ihimaera, these one-sided perceptions are wrong. Even Jimmy Heremaia in "Catching Up" realises that "debiting" his Maori side while "crediting" the Pakeha side is not a satisfactory existence (*Whanau*, p. 36):

> Then the old woman looked into his face and imprisoned him in her eyes.
>
> —Aah, aah, she breathed. Ka pai e tama. Ka pai. Kua u nei koe ki tena taumata o te matauranga.
>
> Jimmy could not look away. He saw a flicker of puzzlement cross quickly over the old woman's eyes likc a shadow.
>
> —I'm sorry, he answered. I don't understand. I don't understand Maori.
>
> The look in the old woman's eyes bruised him ... He had been racing all these years. He had caught up, yes. He had won, but he had also lost. (*The New Net Goes Fishing*, pp. 61–2)

As Alistair Fox comments, in summary: "for the new generation, success merely in Pakeha terms is not enough if Maori identity is lost."[36]

While it could be argued that Ihimaera holds up, as examples for young Maori to emulate, characters who attain individual successes, such as Rongo Mahana and Hepa Walker in *Whanau*, George in "Clenched Fist" and "Tent on the Home Ground", Jimmy Heremaia in "Catching Up", even Miriama in "The Escalator", and Tama Mahana in *The Matriarch*, they are not all shown to be biculturally integrated. In further differentiating these characters who achieve their dreams, Ihimaera allows the reader the choice of which characters could truly be said to be biculturally integrated. This choice is limited, however, for as Michael King notes, the writer through authorial intrusion and prompting makes his preferences obvious: "He stands at the shoulder of the reader and tells him how to react, how to think and feel about the characters and the village."[37] Thus when Christopher's grandfather recalls to Matiu (the same Matiu of "Yellow Brick Road"), "Twenty years ... Twenty years" and asks "But were they worth it, son? Were they? Were they?" one cannot but agree with Matiu and say "Yes, ... I think so" (*The New Net Goes Fishing*, p. 199).

But even without Ihimaera's prompting, the reader is still aware of a distinction between the group of characters like Tama Mahana in *The Matriarch*, George in both "Clenched Fist" and "Tent on the Home Ground", Rongo Mahana, Andrew Whatu, and Pene in *Whanau*, and the other group exemplified by Jimmy Heremaia in "Catching Up", Watene in "The House with Sugarbag Windows", and Hepa Walker in *Whanau*—in spite of the fact that they are all portrayed by Ihimaera as either having realised their individual dreams or on the verge of attaining them. The distinction between the two groups is based on the different degree of bicultural integration each has achieved. Such a state is not to be identified with the achievements of dreams alone.

On the other hand, not one of Ihimaera's characters who is a failure or a drop-out is shown to be biculturally integrated. Assuredly, Ihimaera believes that success in the Pakeha world enhances a character's chances of being biculturally integrated, but he does not see such success as a sufficient cause. Rather, he views economic, academic, and social successes merely as means to the ultimate goal of bicultural integration — in so far as such successes tend to lessen the frustration and alienation which failure in Pakeha terms can cause in the Maori.

Although Ihimaera captures the dilemma and alienation of those characters who are failures and drop-outs with pathos, it is evident that he disapproves of their response to post-colonial problems. Through characters like Api in "Clenched Fist" and "Tent on the Home Ground", Koro, Rose, Thelma, Sambo, and Jonny-Mack in "The Kids Downstairs", Ihimaera exposes the futility of mouthing Black-American slogans and living an aimless existence as solutions to that alienation. Api takes an extremist stance, as Peter points out, because he had failed to realise his dreams: "You see racism in everything .... The system as you call it. Everything. And only because you haven't been able to make it" (*The New Net Goes Fishing*, p. 150). Although Ihimaera uses Api conveniently and unobtrusively to challenge the popular historical notion of Abel Tasman "discovering" an area already inhabited, the belligerent exchanges between Api and Peter serve the literary purpose of setting the scene for Ihimaera to explore the separatist ideology which a lot of radical Maori are advocating.

Ihimaera doubts that the separatist policy is a solution to the problems, for as George tells Api in "Clenched Fist": "I don't think you realise what you're doing or what you really want. Get back our Maoritanga, yes. But don't divide us in the process" (*The New Net Goes Fishing*, p. 41). This echoes Hepa Walker's comments in *Whanau*:

> You'd think they would know better than to accuse the Pakeha for all their "problems" or to say that these are due to a "White racist system" .... What do these kids *really* want? Separatism? They're sure causing it with all their moans and menacing talk. They're promoting discrimination, not solving it, and they're causing ill-feeling between Maori and Pakeha and

> also between Maori and Maori.
> (*Whanau*, pp. 92 – 3)

Ihimaera sees biculturalism as the only viable alternative to separatism for Maori. In "The Kids Downstairs", by contrasting the set of characters who have made it in the Pakeha world with those who have not, he shows an instance where success, in terms of this criterion, creates a sense of bicultural integration. Rangi is Maori, a Civil Servant married to a Pakeha. In Ihimaera's view, Rangi has found his footing in the Pakeha world, for not only is the mixed marriage symbolic of the biculturalism he advocates, it also signifies Rangi's acceptance and integration into Pakeha society. The kids downstairs, Koro, Rose, Thelma, Sambo, and Jonny-Mack, however, are another proposition. They are also Maori, but shiftless and irresponsible — irresponsible not only in not taking their jobs seriously, (this attitude resulting in the sack for Sambo), but also in spending whatever money comes their way in drinking sprees and having fun. Even when they are on the brink of bankruptcy, "they continued to go out to the movies and the pub and to have their parties during the weekend" (*The New Net Goes Fishing*, p. 92).

Ihimaera describes with dripping irony the young people's repetitious use of "not to worry." The kids are worried neither about their desperate economic situation nor about their rootlessness:

> They had still not learnt anything, the kids. They were as careless as ever, as "not to worry" as ever. The only way they knew of not worrying was to walk away from their problems and leave them behind — the bills, the responsibilities, everything — and start up somewhere else until the accumulation of worries compelled them to move again. (*The New Net Goes Fishing*, p. 96)

They are content to drift on the brink of society, neither part of society, nor outside it. In Ihimaera's view, these characters are too rootless and too unconcerned about their future or society's to be biculturally integrated.

But they are still Maori, as much as Rangi is, and Ihimaera has Rangi align himself with them in an exchange with the landlord. By contrasting the remarks of the landlord about Koro and his friends with the remarks about Rangi, Ihimaera shows the two faces of biculturalism as integration. He has the landlord "mumble to himself": "This is the last time I'll ever let a place of mine to Maoris."

> —Now wait a minute, Rangi said. I'm a Maori too, you know.
>
> The landlord looked at him, astonished. His mouth fell open, his cheeks flushed and his eyelids began to beat fast like batwings.
>
> —Oh, but you're *different*, he smiled. You're married to Mrs Johnson. (*The New Net Goes Fishing*, p. 98)

Ihimaera views biculturalism as a matter of attitude. Rangi is different because success in the Pakeha world coupled with marriage to a Pakeha has made him acceptable within the new society; in other words, he is culturally integrated. The landlord's reaction to Rangi, however, shows Ihimaera's awareness of the pejorative application of biculturalism. The racist condescension implicit in the landlord's definition of *different*—"Oh, but you're *different* [because] you're married to [a Pakeha] Mrs Johnson"—exposes Ihimaera's unease about the popular application of "bicultural integration", and its confusion with the concept of assimilation.

It could be argued (as Maori activists, particularly Te Ahi Kaa—the Keepers of the Fire—do) that such integration presupposes a loss of individuality as a Maori or a Pacific Islander. Ihimaera does not agree. He believes that one can be biculturally integrated and still remain either a Pakeha or a Maori. As Hepa Walker says in *Whanau*:

> It isn't as logical as people think, to assume that if you walk into a Pakeha life you walk away from a Maori life. That if you credit yourself in

> the European world you debit somewhere in the Maori world. (*Whanau*, p. 36)

But Ihimaera accepts that the magnitude of change already wrought in the Maori psyche is formidable. He also believes that while certain aspects of the culture could be salvaged, there are, however, some losses that are irreversible. And there are other losses that are both inevitable and necessary, if the Maori is to adapt to the new world. The culture itself must be adaptable, must be subject to change like everything else. In a bicultural context, each culture is open to influence from the other: "Maori people will have to begin to understand and to have more grace about the creative spirit of Pakeha people. We are not the only ones who will interpret our culture . . . now or in the future."[38]

What of the question of Rangi's Maoriness being rendered invisible to the landlord by his "integration" into Pakeha society? Ihimaera is of the view that Rangi's anonymity in this situation should be seen as similar to the anonymity of New Zealanders of either Scottish or Dutch origins, who both remain Pakeha while still retaining some of their ancestral links. [39]

As already mentioned, Ihimaera sees success in Pakeha terms as a means of achieving bicultural integration. Whereas such a success is not equal to biculturalism, a failure in the Pakeha world most often leads to non-integration for most Maori. Ihimaera touches on some of the reasons for the non-realisation of the dream for some of these Maori kids. With the urban drift, Ihimaera says that a lot of Maori children were thrown into the Pakeha world without adequate preparation because their parents were themselves bewildered by Pakeha values, as Charlie Whatu explains to his son:

> I know in my heart that I'm Maori. The world hadn't changed too much when I was a boy, so my whole upbringing was Maori. But you? Well, you live in a Pakeha world and perhaps your Mum and me should have taught you more about your own people. Except that we could

> see it would be no use. You're a throwback, son. You feel the old Maori in your blood and it fights with your Pakeha learning. You have to make your own decision about who and what you are. Maybe you'll be able to live in both worlds without feeling a stranger in either .... Whatever happens, I can't help you and I feel sorry. (*Whanau*, p. 68)

These children are then left to plot their own destinies without adequate parental guidance. For their parents to have guided them, in their own ignorance, would have been tantamount to the blind leading the blind. Whereas in the villages Maori children were free to roam from house to house, to eat, play, and fight with each other, some of these children are confronted with an absolutely incompatible set of values when they step into the Pakeha world. They cannot comprehend their Pakeha neighbours' obsession, for instance, with protecting their privacy—an unfamiliar notion of self-containment in terms of territory and time:

> [Jack Simmons] knows it is too much to expect that the Heremaia children would go to bed so early. Heavens, he is lucky that the tribe has not invaded his house yet! He winces to himself. (*Pounamu, Pounamu*, p. 42)

In school the children are faced with the complex tangle called education, which most feel they cannot unravel:

> Right from the beginning, getting educated had seemed like a marathon most of the other kids had already begun while he was still approaching the starting line. Even then they seemed to have the right equipment—track shoes, good coaching and the encouragement of their parental onlookers—while he stood there waiting in his bare feet and bewilderment. (*The New Net Goes Fishing*, p. 46)

Ihimaera indicates that at this early period the parents often spoke Maori as their first language in the home:

> Mum and Dad .... They'd had no formal education, could barely write a sentence of English and their sole book was a Bible they could read only haltingly and with much difficulty. Their language was composed of broken English and broken gestures. (*The New Net Goes Fishing*, pp. 47–8)

Consequently the English the children were exposed to in class had little in common, either syntactically or phonetically, with that spoken by their parents and elders. Jimmy in "Catching Up" saw English language at school as "incomprehensible chatter which surrounded him" and which sounded "strange to his ears" (*The New Net Goes Fishing*, p. 46). The children had to contend with such problems as grammatical faults and first-language interference. Added to these was the fact that some Pakeha teachers did not appreciate the social and psychological tensions which the children were experiencing. These teachers, having been themselves taught to be fair to all their wards and to treat all their pupils equally, would not even be aware of nor recognise the peculiar needs of the Maori children in their care:

> He'd been the only Maori in his class and had again been the least qualified of a magnificently-endowed field. However, what he did not have in natural ability, he made up with in plain mule-headed stubbornness. He clenched his teeth. All he wanted to do was keep up, keep abreast, keep going... But no amount of forcing could get him through University Entrance.
>
> "I'm sick of failing exams, Mum." (*The New Net Goes Fishing*, p. 56)

At the time that assimilation was urged as the only course in education, most Pakeha did not fully realise how difficult it was for the Maori children to fit into an alien, Pakeha system, and equated poor academic performance by Maori children with dull-wittedness. In Ihimaera's view, it was only the "determined push" by some Maori parents that kept their children from dropping out:

> It hadn't helped when he heard a teacher say:
>
> —I just cannot imagine why the Maori in my class are so hopeless. I am beginning to doubt if they possess any intelligence at all. He'd felt his heart thudding with rage. Then he'd wondered if it was true. He'd asked his mother.
>
> —You tell that teacher to stick his words up his bum, she'd sworn. You tell him to meet us on our home ground, in our own language, and we'll soon see who's intelligent and who isn't. (*The New Net Goes Fishing*, p. 50)

In a world where it was a feat for a Maori kid to get through high school and pass School Certificate as Jimmy does in "Catching Up", and where the easiest way out was to get a job, it needed the constant prodding of parents for some of the Maori kids to keep on:

> Although his jump was ungainly, legs and arms flailing, he made it, scraping through School Certificate with the bare minimum: 200 marks .... Then he had started looking for a job.
>
> —Oh no you don't, Mum said.
>
> —But I've finished now, Mum.
>
> —Oh no you haven't. We got to think about University Entrance now.
>
> —I'll never make *that*, Mum.
>
> .... After you get your University Entrance, then you can leave school.
>
> —But that's what you said when I was going for School Certificate, Mum.
>
> —So what! I've changed my mind!
>
> (*The New Net Goes Fishing*, p. 55)

Ihimaera implies that, if left alone, virtually all the Maori children would prefer to drop out of school. And it is a short hop from dropping out of school to drugs: "I think they went down to Wellington last week to pick up your cousin Raina. They say she's back on the drugs again" (*The Matriarch*, p. 85); or forming gangs, and committing crimes: "Good old Sam, he went to Wellington, bashed a taxi-driver over the head and ended up singing the jail-house blues" (*Whanau*, p. 57). Defeated by the city, such people had to take one of two options. They could swallow their pride and humiliation and head for the village, as Sam Walker (above) and Mattie Jones did in *Whanau*:

> Remembering those few months, those good months, when she and George lived together in a small flat in Newtown .... And then the long lonely times of waiting for George, always waiting ... And knocking on door after door, doing the rounds of the party houses, trying to find him ... moving through grey days and morning sickness. Alone, but not alone ... Refusing help. Too proud to admit to her boss why she is always late for work. Not letting Mum and Dad know about Kara ... And finally, forgetting pride. Ringing home. —Dad? Dad? Please come and get me. (*Whanau*, pp. 60–1)

Or they could form gangs and indulge in petty larcenies. Whichever of these options people took, it still boils down to the same basic issue, which is that they are failures. I believe that Ihimaera makes a distinction between the characters who positively attempt to make their lives better, and the fritterers: "They're all wasters around here, wasting away good sunny days" (*Whanau*, p. 65).

Ihimaera's *The New Net Goes fishing* attempts to correct what he says was the "mismatch" of the "pastoral" reflected by *Pounamu, Pounamu*, *Tangi*, and to some extent *Whanau*, with what he sees as the actual situation of the Maori people—rootless Maori children drifting aimlessly in urban centres with the misguided notion that they are having fun; some parents venting their frustrations on their children by brutalising them. It is obvious that if the kids in "Passing

Time" were in a rural environment, their concept of having fun would be different from "hassling the police and being hassled by them." Ihimaera's short stories "Passing Time" and "The Kids Downstairs", among others, make social statements and ask the question of what degree of control the parents and society have over the behaviour of these children in urban environments. Ihimaera, having established in his earlier works the absolute control that rural societies have over the behaviour of children through their parents and elders, shows through the stories in *The New Net Goes Fishing* just how urgent the problem of urban alienation has become.

As mentioned earlier, Ihimaera's concept of biculturalism is based on a presumption that the individual has to be able to retain and harmonise both cultures. The urban Maori children find it impossible to be biculturally integrated because, in the first instance, they have lost touch with a part of their heritage—the Maori part.

Ihimaera sees biculturalism as a possible answer to the Maori sense of alienation and post-colonial tensions in general, and as a counter to the separatist ideology which some radical Maori are opting for. But he also feels that it is a concept that will be difficult to achieve because it entails the cooperation of both Pakeha and Maori. He believes that Maori issues and problems "can best be resolved within the established system"; and yet, he continues, in an interview with Roy Murphy:

> At the moment we have a situation where the power to determine what is happening in New Zealand rests with Parliament and Pakeha people, and Maori have no power in that sense .... They can be outvoted whenever the European majority wants to. Biculturalism will only work if Maoris implement it and Pakehas allow it. It's an equality of power; that's what biculturalism is all about. Power to make decisions about New Zealand's destiny, a destiny which involves two peoples in the South Pacific.[40]

Ihimaera's admission paradoxically supports the stance of the advocates of separatism such as Atareta Poananga, "who no longer advocates biculturalism since she believes that it offers Maori power-sharing on Pakeha terms."[41] In a published interview, Poananga enlarges:

> Whatever the Pakeha decides for us it can only ever be on their terms, according to their needs. This means we as Maori, slot into their culturally alien structures. English language, education, culture and religion, are seen as the natural targets of attainment for Maori people . . . . You are socialised from birth into believing everything Maori is bad or inferior. You see there is only one destiny—to be white, to succeed in white things.[42]

She questions Ihimaera's belief that the goal of biculturalism is attainable since, she argues, "if it hasn't been instituted in 150 years it's not going to be now."[43] It was Ihimaera's difficulty in resolving this paradox, allowing that the Maori activists could possibly be right, that led to his self-imposed break and the hiatus in his writing career. George's despair at the end of "Clenched Fist", as he ponders whether Api and his friends are right in their advocacy for separatism, reflects Ihimaera's dilemma. George, like Ihimaera, has tried to have an objective view of society and the "establishment", based on his belief in the concept of biculturalism. This has led to incessant quarrels with Api, his radical friend, but George has come to the conclusion that biculturalism is the answer and that "Api was wrong and he [George] was right" (*New Net Goes Fishing*, p. 41). However, a nasty incident causes George to doubt his earlier conclusion:

> Suddenly, shouting. George turned to look back. The lights had turned green and cars were moving across the intersection . . . . Caught in it was a woman late in crossing. A car was speeding toward her.

> —Get back. Get back you black bitch.
>
> The words cracked above the roar of traffic .... Laughter spilled from the receding car. Amusement in the eyes of bystanders. The woman remained there, bewildered and frightened. A knot of despair tightened in George's stomach. Trembling, he stood there. Was he wrong after all? (*The New Net Goes Fishing*, pp. 41–2)

These doubts that assail George (and, implicitly, Ihimaera) are further explored in "Tent on the Home Ground" as the author analyses the reasons for George not being promoted. George's Pakeha friend, David, agrees with Api that "George should have been promoted", except that Api gives the reason for non-promotion as being that George "is a black man and this is a white system" (*The New Net Goes Fishing*, pp. 148–9). Api further argues: "And does the white man want us in positions of power? Like hell he does." The narrator rationalises, albeit tongue in cheek, that:

> Apparently [George] still didn't fit in, still appeared to lack that special sense of administrative ability and those nebulous qualities which interviewers were instructed to seek out in those applying for promotion. (*The New Net Goes Fishing*, p. 148)

Api, on the other hand, believes that George was being discriminated against because he is Maori:

> You take a good hard look at the system you've created. It's in your image, not ours. Everything about it is white. Religion. Education. Politics. You name it. And I'll bet you there's hardly any of us in it. Why? Because you're scared of us. So you keep us down. At the bottom of the system. (*The New Net Goes Fishing*, p. 149)

The similarities between Api's arguments and those of Atareta Poananga, as noted above, are indicative of Ihimaera's concern that there possibly exists some justification for the stance of the Maori activists.

The hiatus in Ihimaera's writing career "radicalised" his views about contemporary Maori issues and his concept of biculturalism, and edged him closer to the activist camp.

Between the publication of *The New Net Goes Fishing* in 1977 and *The Matriarch* in 1986, Ihimaera wrote an address entitled "Maori life and literature: a sensory perception" for the Turnbull Library, setting out his own personal and political history:

> My father's parents were Perapunahamoa Ihimaera Smiler and Teria Pere. Through my grandfather's mother, Hine Te Ariki, I enter Te Whanau A Apanui; through my great-grandfather, Ihimaera Te Hanene, I am Tuhoe. On my grandmother's side, I am a descendant of Wi Pere. . . .
>
> Political and social reality is a difficult matter to recognise, and we each come to it in different ways. In my case it happened when I was thirteen and I had seen that my birth certificate had my name as Witi Tame Ihimaera (Smiler). . . . I could not remember having heard that name Ihimaera before. My father and I were sitting at home and I asked him: 'What's this name, Ihimaera?' He told me it was our real name, our Maori name. 'Well, why are we known around here as "Smiler"?' My father's reply was: 'When your grandfather was younger, the missionaries couldn't pronounce his name "Ihimaera". So they gave him another name, "Smiler".'
>
> I began to use Ihimaera from then on. It means Ishmael, and it was my greatgrandfather's first name. Ishmael was of the desert people in the Old Testament and it seemed entirely appropriate for me—a wanderer in the desert. The more I dwelt on the 'why' of the name-change the more I began to see the way in which Maori life was under siege.[44]

Ihimaera's Turnbull Library Lecture and two *Listener* editorials are ample testimony of his concern about contemporary issues of relevance to Maori — land rights, urban alienation, high infant mortality rates, and the lack of impetus for educational achievements among Maori children which leads to their early dropping-out from school.

In an editorial titled "The Maori Landscape" Ihimaera writes that Maori culture "needs air to survive, it needs land to stand on. To survive with any strength and beauty it needs more than a cultural renaissance to support it; it needs a cultural revolution."[45]

It requires a "commitment to change, to the alteration of what New Zealanders feel themselves to be, and to the establishment of symbols of culture which we might in time come to hold in common:"[46]

> The irony, of course is that to achieve these things may require what look like "separate" institutions or separate programmes of support — such as Radio Polynesia and Maori language courses in schools. Indeed, the establishment of a new Council for traditional Maori and Polynesian Arts by the Government has already been criticised as being a move towards apartheid. The answer to that criticism is: without a Council we do have apartheid, with it we don't, because, for the first time ever, we have given due recognition to the Maori gifts of culture. Are New Zealanders able to make such a special commitment and accept that some separate devclopment is necessary to the alteration to our direction as a nation?[47]

This sharpened awareness of "the very real social, economic, legal and other problems facing the Maori people today"[48] and Ihimaera's new radical viewpoint are most fully articulated in *The Matriarch* and *The Whale Rider*.

3

Coming to Terms with the New Way: the Radicalisation of Ihimaera's Views in *The Matriarch*

The Matriarch reveals the flowering to full bloom of Ihimaera's social consciousness. It reaffirms Ihimaera's vision of a bicultural New Zealand, his conviction that it is the only viable option for New Zealanders, and for the Maori in particular. Paradoxically, it acknowledges the validity of some of the agitations of Maori activists, and fully represents Maori grief and anger over past injustices conditioned by the nature of the early contacts between Maori and Pakeha. It further explores the concept of biculturalism as a difficult but necessary alternative to separatism.

Ihimaera probes the historical causes of Maori alienation and post-colonial tension, in the firm belief that the acknowledgement by all New Zealanders of these past injustices and problems is essential if they are to be resolved. As Wole Soyinka has said:

> the turning up of the maggot-infested underside of the compost heap ... is a prerequisite of the land's transformation.[1]

Ihimaera constructs an account of the historical origins of the present predicament from a Maori vantage point to counterbalance traditional Pakeha versions that he considers biased. An analysis of Ihimaera's account of the historical origins of Maori grievances is necessary for a comprehension of both his new radical stance and the paradox of his continued advocacy for biculturalism. This chapter will deal with Ihimaera's establishment of a Maori sense of history, and his proposal for coming to terms with the "new way".

The first Europeans encountered a communally based agrarian Maori society, as Bill Pearson describes it:

> We should recall that in pre-European times the Maori were an industrious people, that their main energies went to producing food and clothing and shelter with primitive implements.[2]

Ihimaera concurs, saying: "The matriarch's people were renowned fishermen and agriculturists" (*The Matriarch*, p. 46). He quotes Joseph Barrow Montefiore, Sydney merchant, as claiming in 1838 that: "Their potatoes are cultivated better than those grown by many of the settlers in New South Wales". But, Ihimaera continues, "with the change to sheep farming, on sheep runs which were already leased or sold to the Pakeha, the agricultural basis of the people collapsed" (p. 46).

By 1896, says Pearson, the Maori race was thought to be dying, and the formerly "industrious" Maori had gotten "the reputation among the Pakeha for indolence, improvidence, shiftlessness and unreliability."[3] Ihimaera's fiction attempts to explain what had happened in the interim to engender such a colossal reversal in the Maori psyche.

The way Ihimaera restructures and uses the accepted historical accounts of the first contact between the European and the Maori provides the first focus for this study. This chapter will also explore the ambivalent education of Tamatea into both the matriarch's understanding of the Maori sense of alienation and her vision of ways to right it. It also examines his discovery of, and education into, her darker side—and the use or misuse of traditional occult powers. A section of this chapter will deal with the controversy about Ihimaera's concept of biculturalism and its reappraisal which his most recent novel, *The Whale Rider*, seems to imply.

The Historical Background and Ihimaera's Revisionism

The European discovery of New Zealand on 6 October 1769 by Captain James Cook, and subsequent European contacts with the Maori in the years between 1779 and 1840, saw "the gradual coming of the Pakeha—first as whaler, ... then as flax trader ... tree feller, evangelist and, finally, settler and farmer" (*The Matriarch*, p. 46). Bassett notes that:

> the first European traders, like the explorers, were not interested in living permanently in New Zealand. They wanted to make profits from the sale of natural resources like flax, timber, sealskins or whale oil. These products fetched good prices in Europe ..."[4]

However, Pakeha eventually started settling in New Zealand. This early contact between European and Maori is intriguing from the literary perspective, for, as Lawrence Jones says in another connection: "if there is only one story, there are two different ways of telling it."[5] One way of telling this particular story is found in the account of a famous Maori chief, Te Horeta Taniwha, as quoted by Judith Bassett in *The Story of New Zealand*, a history intended for use in schools:

> In the days long past, when I was a very little boy, a vessel came to Whitianga ... when our old men saw the ship they said it was a tupua, a god, and the people on board were strange beings. The ship came to anchor, and the boats pulled on shore. As our old men looked at the manner in which they came on shore, the rowers pulling with their backs to the bows of the boat, the old people said, "Yes, it is so: these people are goblins; their eyes are at the back of their heads; they pull on shore with their backs to the land to which they are going .... We were now

> at quiet and peace with them, and they gave us some of the food they had brought on shore with them. Some of this food was very hard, but it was sweet."[6]

But there is more than one "Maori" version of the story. Ihimaera writes, of the earliest contacts:

> All New Zealand schoolchildren are taught about Captain James Cook's discovery of New Zealand and his historic landfall at Poverty Bay in the *Endeavour* in October 1769. They are told that the event was quite glorious .... They are told, to some amusement, that the reaction of the Maori people on the shore was one of awe for the huge white bird, the floating island, and the multicoloured gods who had come on the bird .... But what the schoolchildren are not told is that Cook's first landing was marked by the killing of a Maori called Te Maro, shot through the heart by a musket bullet, Monday 9 October, 1769. Then on the morning of Tuesday 10 October, 1769, another Maori called Te Rakau was shot and killed, and three others were wounded. During the afternoon of the same day a further four Maori were murdered ... and three of their companions were taken captive. Captain James Cook claimed New Zealand for Britain. The *Endeavour* finally left Poverty Bay on Thursday 12 October, 1769. The glorious birth of the nation has the taste of bitter almonds when one remembers that six Maori died so that a flag could be raised. (*The Matriarch*, p. 36–7)

Ihimaera's revisionist version questions the widely held historical beliefs and accounts of the harmonious first contact between the European and Maori. The sharp contrast between this "taste of bitter almonds" version and Te Horeta Taniwha's recollection, of "quiet and peace" and the sharing of "sweet" tasting food, is but one instance of what he views as historical bias: selective attention to the various accounts handed down.

There is also a marked contrast in tone, when Ihimaera describes post-settlement activity in one sweeping sentence; the first Europeans in New Zealand, he says,— whaler, flax trader, evangelist, settler, and farmer—had one thing in mind:

> All these Pakeha strode through the villages, the hundreds of pa sites, smothering the Maori fires and razing the temples of pagan religion. (*The Matriarch*, p. 46)

In his earlier short story, "Tent On the Home Ground," Ihimaera, through the character Api, refutes the claim that Abel Tasman discovered New Zealand, on the basis that what he "discovered" was an area already inhabited—that the credit of "discovery" belongs to Kupe:

> You ask for proof [of racism] and there's so much of it I don't know where to begin.
>
> —Because there isn't any, Peter said.
>
> Api narrowed his eyes. Then he flashed the quick smile of a panther.
>
> —Who discovered New Zealand? he asked Peter.
>
> —Eh? Oh, Abel Tasman, Peter answered startled.
>
> And Api grinned with triumph.
>
> —Man, he said. Your answer is your proof. Long before Abel Tasman got here, Kupe discovered this country. But you've probably never heard of him. After all, he was only a Maori.
>
> Peter reddened with anger.
>
> —Kupe? He's just a legend.
>
> —Your second proof, Api answered. Anything that happened to us you call myth or legend. Anything that happened to you is called history. (*The New Net Goes Fishing*, pp. 149–50)

Ihimaera believes that relegating the story of Kupe to the class of a legend perpetuated the notion that there was no Maori history to talk of until the coming of the Pakeha. He relates the modern Pakeha assumption of a barren historical landscape to earlier attitudes and activities which saw the traducing of a people's entire world view, leading to Maori disillusionment up until the closing years of the nineteenth century. It is evident from the foregoing and from Ihimaera's advocacy of biculturalism that he is not opposing the advent of Pakeha settlers *per se*, but rather the changes wrought in the Maori way of life and what he sees as the distortion of historical facts to accommodate Pakeha perspectives.

Ihimaera acknowledges that some of these changes, such as the introduction of advanced techniques of farming and farm implements, the abolition of such practices as cannibalism, and the reduction in the incidence of intertribal wars, were essentially beneficial to the Maori. But to him, other changes like the destruction of a cultural heritage, land dispossession, and its attendant dissolution of family ties due to urban drift, were very harmful.

Mention should be made of Ihimaera's views on a few other relevant issues of the nineteenth century as a background to appraising his proposed resolution of Maori postcolonial tensions, and his concept of bicultural integration. This is necessary because, in Ihimaera's accounts, these issues are bound together by the process of cause and effect. They include the role of the missionaries, theTreaty of Waitangi and formal settlements, the land wars, the Land Courts, the Te Kooti uprising, and the early attempts to integrate Pakeha and Maori values, as symbolised by the paintings in the meeting-house, Te Rongopai.

Unlike "the traders who did not wish to change Maori society [though] their new goods and techniques did eventually bring about big changes", the missionaries, says Judith Bassett, "did want to change the Maori society."[7] Considering that the aim of these missionaries "was to bring civilization and Christianity to a heathen world," the fact that they "tried consciously to change Maori culture" was inevitable.[8]

As well as causing the destruction of Maori culture and of traditional religious customs, Ihimaera believes that the evangelists often initiated conflict:

> There had already been violent clashes and slayings: Maori and Maori, Maori and Pakeha. The former were continuations of earlier conflicts in line with the concept of utu. Those between Maori and Pakeha were frequently caused by the violation of the laws of tapu—even by the evangelists. (*The Matriarch*, p. 47)

In other instances, he relates through Tama, the missionaries aggravated existing conflicts:

> . . . there is one point in John Lawrence's delivery which I would agree with and which needs further amplification. This is the role of the church in extending the conflict between Maori and Pakeha over the spiritual domain. Possibly my visit surprised John . . . for I am sure that he would have elaborated on the role of the Christian religion in aggravating Maori-Pakeha relations. It wasn't good enough just to take away our lands. Oh no, the Pakeha had to take away our souls too! Not only did we have to give up our physical world; we had to give up our spiritual world as well. (*The Matriarch*, p. 71)

Ihimaera particularly views it as "intolerable", in John Lawrence's words, "that Christian ministers could equate [the Maori] people with savagery and paganism and therefore quite blithely establish a religion that was just as savage and as pagan" (*The Matriarch*, p. 69). The Maori, he asserts, places a high premium on spiritual well-being because it governs almost all aspects of life. He quotes the late Te Kani Te Ua as saying that "while the Maori people might be called a barbaric and savage race [their] knowledge and conception of the spirit world show a high plane of thought similar to the philosophical speculations of the earliest Greek philosophers—Empedocles, Anaximander and others" (*The Matriarch*, p. 252).

Ihimaera also remarks that the Christian concept of retribution for sins committed differs from that of the Maori. This, he says in Tama's voice, influences the way the two peoples perceive issues:

> The Christian was punished in an after life; the Maori was punished here and now in this world. This is why the Maori has always been more careful than the Pakeha in observing religious customs. (*The Matriarch*, p. 256)

Some of Ihimaera's writings show that, while the coming of the Pakeha precipitated a great number of changes, the extent of change varies. Some events, such as the signing of the Treaty of Waitangi, have had a chain-reaction effect of such magnitude that the reverberations are still felt keenly in Maori consciousness. Ihimaera's incessant reference to the Treaty implies that Maori land issues and consequently Maori alienation cannot be adequately discussed without recourse to the Treaty. If there is anything that exemplifies Lawrence Jones's comment, mentioned earlier, that where there is one story there is more than one way of telling it, it is the Treaty of Waitangi.[9]

Judith Bassett writes that it was, among other things, the flurry of land speculations and activities of Edward Gibbon Wakefield, his brother Captain Arthur Wakefield and other land speculators between 1838 and 1840 that prompted William Hobson to "summon Maori chiefs to a meeting at Waitangi on 5 February 1840" and which led to the signing of the Treaty on 6 February 1840.[10]

Ihimaera's ambivalent attitude to the Treaty reflects the complexity of the arguments about it. D. F. McKenzie claims "that Maori assent to the treaty became the substantive ground of British sovereignty over New Zealand."[11] This supports Ihimaera's view in *The Matriarch* that "It was the instrument by which the British decided to extend their sovereignty to New Zealand" (p. 73); and that the organised

Pakeha settlement and colonisation which started in 1840 was consequent on the Treaty (*The Matriarch*, p. 238). But there is another body of opinion. This, as acknowledged by McKenzie, "regards the treaty as having no effect and British sovereignty as arising rather from the occupation and settlement of lands inhabited by uncivilized native peoples."[12] What everyone agrees on, however, is that the Treaty is open to innumerable interpretations. Bassett mentions "doubts over the true meaning of the Treaty of Waitangi".[13] Apart from it being difficult to understand, she continues, it was drawn up in a hurry, by a man who was not a lawyer and had no training in such matters.

Ihimaera's belief, as expressed in *The Matriarch*, that "the Treaty has never had any status in domestic or international law" and that "the Pakeha signed it knowing it was worthless" (p. 73), is linked with the problems of the multiplicity of versions of the treaty and of interpretative bias arising from its various different wordings. Bassett reports that "the Maoris at Waitangi signed the Maori version, some Waikato chiefs later signed the English version" and that "the two versions are not exactly the same." McKenzie, writing on the same issue, points out that there are many English versions:

> Hobson also sent abroad ... five English versions of the Treaty. There are minor differences in three of them, but the other two bear a different date, differ from the others in the wording of their preamble, and differ critically from each other in the second article. [14]

Quoting Ruth Ross, McKenzie enlarges: "The extant Maori version, the actual treaty as signed by the chiefs on 6 February, is not a translation of any of these five English versions, nor is any of the English ones a translation from the Maori." [15] The implication of the above, according to Ross, is that the Maori version is the real Treaty of Waitangi; this accounts for Ihimaera's insistence that the Treaty is legally binding.

Ihimaera's argument that the Pakeha signed the Treaty knowing it was worthless emphasizes his opinion that the Treaty was based on deceit. McKenzie argues that the signatories to the Treaty "could not have read [the Treaty] even if they had known the [English] language."[16] Having made the point about European assumptions about the comprehension, status, and binding power of the written word, and having stressed the questionable status of the Maori "translations", McKenzie remarks:

> Without begging any questions about Pakeha intent to deceive, even the Maori language itself was used against the Maori. First, much of the detail of the English draft was presumed by Williams to be inexpressible in Maori translation. Second, the forms of Maori used to communicate Pakeha intentions were . . . not indigenous Maori but protestant Pakeha missionary Maori. . . . Not only the concepts, but many of the words, for all their Maori form, were English.[17]

McKenzie further argues that: "By choosing not to use either 'mana' or 'rangatiratanga' to indicate what the Maori would exchange for 'all the rights and privileges of British subjects', Williams muted the sense, plain in English, of the Treaty as a document of political appropriation." In McKenzie's view, "had any Maori heard that he was giving up his mana or rangatiratanga he could never have agreed to the treaty's terms."[18]

Coupled with the above issue is another piece of background information: Bassett agrees with Ihimaera that Henry Williams, who translated the Maori version, "was very concerned about protecting all the land he had bought. Williams claimed ownership of 11,000 acres."[19] Ihimaera mentions that Reverend Archdeacon Henry Williams, missioner for the Church Missionary Society, in answer to accusations of having appropriated Maori lands, replied:

> . . . the missionaries had done sterling services in New Zealand, they had laboured long hours

> in the service of others, that he himself had a family to support—eleven children in all—and, why, surely the land he had was not excessive given the fact that it would have to be divided eleven ways on his death? (*The Matriarch*, p. 72)

Ihimaera thus implies that it is unlikely that a man like Henry Williams, with vested interest in Maori lands, would be fair in the translations, particularly when he had to improvise and coin new non-Maori words like "Kawanatanga" (Government). But most importantly, he feels that the Maori have been deceived:

> The Crown said that all property belonged to the Maori and could not be taken without our consent and without payment. Land was made available for European settlement, but the interests of Maori owners were protected by restricting to the Government the right to purchase their land. Other intrinsic rights were also guaranteed .... The Pakeha signed it knowing it was worthless .... For most assuredly *you*, Pakeha, began taking the land from us as you were signing your worthless Treaty. (*The Matriarch*, pp. 73–4)

McKenzie's analysis of Pakeha assumptions about Maori attitudes, and of early Maori comprehension of English, lends support to Ihimaera's view of implied deceit. Both emphasize the oral nature of Maori culture and its transmission. The Treaty, in McKenzie's opinion,

> offers a prime example of European assumptions about the comprehension, status and binding power of written statements and written consent on the one hand as against the flexible accommodations of oral consensus on the other. [20]

He argues that it is absurd for Europeans to think that what took Europe two millennia to accomplish—conversion from an oral culture to a written one—had been achieved in a mere twenty-five years in New Zealand.

McKenzie's premise is that there would be a cultural reluctance to "shift from memory to written record ... to surrender the relativities of time, place and person in an oral culture to the presumed fixities of the written or printed word."[21] But most especially, he argues that:

> Maori understanding of the treaty was undoubtedly formed by their sense that the independence (the rangatiratanga) and the sovereignty (the mana) they had affirmed in 1835 and reaffirmed by further subscriptions as late as 1839, was not nullified by the treaty ... for the Maori one document did not supersede the other: they lived together, one complementing the other.[22]

This, McKenzie believes, is the basis of Maori assent to the Treaty.

Ihimaera asserts, through Tama, that the Maori chiefs who signed the Treaty, and the present generation of Maori, believe that the Treaty is legally binding on all parties: "All you Pakeha lawyers can argue until the cows come home that the Treaty wasn't a legal document but we believe it is" (*The Matriarch*, p. 73). It is thus the differences in perception occasioned by the inherent cultural differences between the Maori and Pakeha, exemplified by their different perspectives on both the Treaty and other issues concerning land, that eventually led to the land wars.[23]

Ihimaera's fictions, his *New Zealand Listener* editorials and extra-literary activities collectively indicate that, more than any other factor, land issues are at the root of most Maori versus Pakeha conflicts, and that the Maori's sense of frustration and alienation is best perceived as their expressed grief for lost lands.[24] The stridency evident in Ihimaera's writings about Maori land issues, particularly in *The Matriarch*, is caused by his belief that land dispossession is at the heart of the post-colonial distress of the Maori people. He claims that "before the arrival of European settlers, the Maori had 66 million acres of land, today they have less than three million" (*The Matriarch*, p. 235). This is a claim that some disagree with.[25]

Ihimaera views the effects of this landlessness as three-dimensional—economic, social, and cultural. Having mentioned the varied guises under which the Maori lost their lands, he observes that, apart from the apparent economic loss to those whose lands are forcibly taken without compensation, where a member of a family single-handedly sells the family land in opposition to the wishes of other members of the family, there is bound to be acrimony, which will in all probability lead to an ostracising of the culprit (*The Matriarch*, pp. 319–20). Other ramifications of such an event would be the weakening of family ties, the splintering of the whanau and the depriving of some members of the family (particularly if it is a very large family) of a means of livelihood—the farmland. It is the reduction in agricultural productivity due to reduced farmland that has forced the younger members to *drift* to the urban areas:

> Yes, it is true—the land has been taken and where there is no land the people must leave and find new livelihood in the cities to the north and to the south. Gone, gone, they have gone, the iwi from the land. (*The Matriarch*, p. 50)

Linked to the economic effects are the social and cultural consequences. Ihimaera acknowledges that the predilection of the government which is predominantly Pakeha would be to buy land for Pakeha settlers; also that the government would be likely to pass legislation that would make this task less onerous. But he sympathizes with the Maori stance:

> The views of Maori and Pakeha about the future of the country were absolutely incompatible. The government attempted to buy more and more land, urgently needed by the Pakeha settlers; the Maori people considered these attempts to be against their express wish to retain the land. (*The Matriarch*, p. 238)

Despite the opposition of some tribes to the sale of land, the sales continued: "from the very beginning of organised

Pakeha colonisation in 1840, many Maori tribes had opposed the sale of land" (*The Matriarch*, p. 238). Since not everyone would agree to sell their lands, those who were willing to sell would most probably be censured, leading to quarrels: "tribes were divided as individuals defied chiefs to sell land" (*The Matriarch*, p. 239).

Ihimaera views the social consequences of such defiance as grave — a total breakdown of traditional norms. He argues that the urban drift of young Maori was consequent on these economic and social effects, resulting in the cultural dislocation discussed earlier. In Ihimaera's view, the opposition to the sale of land, in some cases, stemmed from the elders' knowledge of the long term consequences on the younger generation of such sales. John Lawrence tells Tama Mahana in *The Matriarch*:

> Your grandmother was one of the old people who could see what was happening. She realised that it was important to try to bring the land back into Maori hands because otherwise the young would continue to leave it. (*The Matriarch*, p. 232)

Ihimaera realises that economic reality is always inextricably entwined with urban drift, and so it is with the postcolonial Maori people. He also believes that the centrality of land to all the tensions and conflicts between Pakeha and Maori is due to the Maori's deep-rooted spiritual attachment to the land, which many Pakeha find incongruous. In the words of Brian J. Murton:

> While land can mean many things to Maori New Zealanders an important dimension of Maori land is the spiritual attachment which its owners feel for it, not as mere economic space, but as place. This feeling for land clashes with the way land is viewed by New Zealand's dominant Pakeha culture ... but perhaps even more significant was that the settlers, creatures of their culture, valued land in terms of the productive use man could make of it. From the classical

> economic perspective, land was only beautiful which was most fruitful.[26]

Murton's comment is echoed in the view of Te Matakite, the group that organized the land march from Te Hapua to Wellington in 1975, as Ihimaera reports it in *The Matriarch*:

> land means much more to the Maori people than it does to any other New Zealander. To them it has a deep spiritual value. You can realise then the frustration the Maori people have had over the last 150 years as they have seen their lands gradually fall out of their hands. (*The Matriarch*, p. 235)

The colonial and post-colonial Pakeha domination of both government and the judiciary, Ihimaera alleges, coupled with a thirst for arable lands by Pakeha settlers, meant that it was easy for Maori land to pass into Pakeha hands. Ihimaera argues in *The Matriarch* that, deprived of their only source of sustenance, young Maori had no alternative but to drift to the city in search of a means of livelihood. He says that: "The Maoris have no other earthly possessions than the land which they inherited from their ancestors" (*The Matriarch*, p. 333).

Ihimaera recognises very many factors as responsible for the colossal reversal of Maori land ownership from Maori to Pakeha. The first obvious factor was the greed of a few individuals for the valuable things that the Europeans exchanged for land:

> The matriarch's own great-great-uncle was one of the first Pakeha to own land in the Gisborne district, the block known as "Pouparae" which he acquired on 18 December 1839: 1004 acres in exchange for £80 cash, four double-barrelled fowling pieces, 40 shirts, 36 axes, 32 plane irons, 60 blankets, 36 iron pots, 24 hoes, 400 lbs of tobacco, 36 hatchets, 130 razors, 30 knives, 40 spades, and 22 pairs of scissors. (*The Matriarch*, p. 46)

Ihimaera mentions that, traditionally, most lands belonged to either the community as a whole or to individual families, with the result that, often, no one person could sell a piece of land without the consent of the other members of the whanau or the chief. Land legislation then became a factor through which the government could ease the acquisition of Maori lands by Pakeha settlers: "... it was the land legislation which had the most disastrous results for the Maoris who became involved. Transactions were swift and shady, the land speeding from beneath the toes of the Maori" (*The Matriarch*, p. 239). Ihimaera sees the land legislations as part of a wider pattern of deceit through which the Pakeha gained control of Maori land:

> Under the Native Land Acts of 1862 and 1865 the Crown's right of pre-emption was abolished, a Maori Land Court was established to individualise Maori land titles, and European settlers were permitted to purchase land directly from the individuals named in the court's orders. Oh, it could make you weep, but the Pakeha foisted this one on the Maori by claiming that this land legislation was part of a wider policy designed to fulfil the promise of the Treaty of Waitangi to grant Maori the rights and privileges of European citizens. (*The Matriarch*, p. 239)

A sense of gross injustice, in the use of the arena of justice—the courts—to deprive the Maori of their land, pervades Ihimaera's *The Matriarch*, particularly with regard to the functions of Native Land Courts. In Ihimaera's view, by using the courts to individualise Maori lands, the Pakeha effectively denied the Maori any legal redress. He reports the words of Wi Pere in Parliament, from the record in Hansard:

> Another evil is that, if one of the Natives sells his share to a European, the shares of the whole of the others who have not sold go to the European as well. By this means the lands of some people

> are taken from them unjustly. (*The Matriarch*, p. 320)

Since it was the courts that individualised the lands in the first place, there was no remedy for the Maori so injured in "the arena of the Maori Land Courts"; for the "Europeans, being the superior race, superior in education, ... took advantage of our ignorance" (*The Matriarch*, p. 320). The Maori thus lost faith in the Pakeha concept of justice:

> Maori tribal lands from the very beginning, even before the ink was dry on the document, have been illegally taken, granted, sold, leased and wrongly withheld, misused and misplaced. There have been losses of forestry rights, mineral rights, fishing rights and Maori tribal cultural rights. (*The Matriarch*, p. 73)

Ihimaera sees Maori insurgencies of the nineteenth century—the Hauhau war, the land wars, the Te Kooti uprising—as resulting first from the loss of land, and then from the failure of justice for the Maori. The Maori believed, in the words of Whina Cooper as she appears in *The Matriarch*, that "not only do we lose everything if we lose our land. We also become nothing" (p. 236). When the land was "illegally taken" in the nineteenth century, and particularly as the Treaty on the basis of which they felt British sovereignty was established was now an issue of controversy, the ancestors decided to go to war. As Whina is also quoted as saying: "Far better to die on land that the Pakeha has taken from us. We must fight, fight, fight" (*The Matriarch*, p. 236). Ihimaera speaks for Maori in general when he says "our forefathers had fought and died last century to rectify the inconsistencies and injustices that the Treaty embodies" (*The Matriarch*, p. 73). The land wars were waged to prevent further Maori lands from being "swallowed up by the greedy Pakeha speculators" and also to prevent the customs and traditions of the Maori from being "trampled on by the Pakeha" (*The Matriarch*, pp. 73–4). However, the land wars, rather than stem the change of ownership of lands from Maori to Pakeha, actually accelerated it, especially with the land confiscations which came in the aftermath of the war.

In Ihimaera's view, these wars which lasted from 1860–1881, and which the Maori lost, gave the government the opportunity to appropriate more Maori lands: "altogether 3,215,172 acres of Maori land were confiscated in the Waikato, Taranaki and the Bay of Plenty to pay for Maori insurgency" (*The Matriarch*, p. 239). The government's initial intention was to confiscate only the lands belonging to the rebels. However, in returning some lands, the government realised that the task of winnowing was almost impossible; it then

> proposed that the loyal chiefs should magnanimously and voluntarily hand over blocks of land in Poverty Bay, Wairoa and on the East Coast as *representing* the land interests of the rebels; in turn, the Crown would waive any claim to rebel interests outside the blocks so ceded .... So the Maori who had fought for the Crown were confronted with the humiliation of handing over to the Crown tribal land as the fine for the rebels whom *they*, the loyalists, had fought against .... This was the way in which the Pakeha rewarded this friendliness. (*The Matriarch*, pp. 240–1)

Ihimaera's view of these past actions by the government provides another instance of the importance of the issue of land in the post-colonial context. As the matriarch tells her grandson, "what happened to Te Kooti is what has happened to all of us" (*The Matriarch*, p. 133). In Ihimaera's view, all these issues—the role of missionaries, the Treaty of Waitangi and formal settlement, the land wars, the land courts, and the punitive response to the Te Kooti uprising—have all, collectively, contributed to modern Maori disenchantment. The modern land marches are an expression of protest at injustice that has its roots in the nineteenth century. Ihimaera sees the Te Kooti uprising as the morally-justified reaction of a man deprived of justice. The "Song of Te Kooti" told by the matriarch, and the analysis of "the Matawhero Retaliation", are attempts to present an alternative viewpoint to the prevailing assumptions on these topics, in accordance with Ihimaera's concept that:

> All truth is fiction really, for the teller tells it as he sees it, and it might be different from some other teller. This is why histories often vary, depending on whether you are the conqueror or not. (*The Matriarch*, p. 403)

Other writers have referred to these incidents as "the Te Kooti rebellion" and "the Matawhero massacre", and Ihimaera quotes even Sir Apirana Ngata as saying:

> With the end of the Hauhau War ... we reach the last landmark in the historical past of the Maori race. Te Kooti is the last and greatest representative of the worst side of the Maori character—its subtlety, cunning and treachery; its cruelty and love of bloodshed; and its immorality and fanaticism. His character had no relieving trait; no anecdotes of liberality or magnanimity extenuate the horror we must feel for him. It was not to be wondered at; he was not a chief. In all his schemes and undertakings there is lacking the kindly liberality, the magnanimity, the true dignity of the Maori chief. (*The Matriarch*, p. 196)

In the "Song of Te Kooti", Ihimaera makes a distinction between the two points of view, Pakeha and Maori, on Matawhero. He says that "when [John Lawrence] refers to the 'Matawhero massacre' what he really is referring to is Te Kooti Rikirangi's *retaliation* against a whole history of Pakeha abuse of Maori people, custom and land" (*The Matriarch*, p. 71). Ihimaera not only justifies Te Kooti's taking up of arms to defend both himself and his followers on the basis of his having been "falsely imprisoned ... and exiled", he mentions that Te Rongopai was established as a "tribute to Te Kooti's struggle to retain Maori identity during the years of the whirlwind" (*The Matriarch*, p. 135). He also portrays Te Kooti as acting in self-defence: "The Pakeha wished to hunt him down like an animal. Only then did he take up arms against Pharaoh and against all Egypt" (*The Matriarch*, p. 134).

Maurice Shadbolt, in *Season of the Jew*, analyses the varied concepts of justice in the Te Kooti affair. Although the accounts by Ihimaera and Shadbolt differ in both the scope and analysis given to some aspects of the Te Kooti uprising, it is pertinent to note that both authors believe Te Kooti to have been treated unjustly in the first instance. The matriarch relates, in Ihimaera's "Song of Te Kooti":

> It was Captain Read who instigated it all to prevent Te Kooti from hurting his own trade .... Ah yes, and the Pakeha also wanted to remove all those who were troublesome and all those who persisted in disturbing the peace of Egypt. (*The Matriarch*, p. 135)

Shadbolt is even more explicit on this score. Read says in *Season of the Jew*: "The sod started out working for me. Here. He could add. Price. Write good English. Deal with skippers. And sell a lion's skin before he'd shot the lion .... He was smart."[27] Te Kooti's crime according to Read was that he turned from a servant into a competitor: "He started his own store across the river .... He took native trade. Even if they didn't like him, they liked his prices."[28] Shadbolt, writing about the lack of justice in Major Biggs's treatment of Te Kooti as a prelude to the eventual revolt, has George Fairweather state: "The more you stir turd, the worse it stinks .... I understand that Read made land available for the settlement at Matawhero on the condition that he was rid of Coates."[29] The real reason Read wanted the banishment of Te Kooti was that, without him, Read would have "no rival in trade."[30]

Both Ihimaera and Shadbolt believe, unequivocally, that there were three major reasons for Te Kooti's deportation and none of them had anything to do with law and justice.

The first was his land. Shadbolt's Fairweather remarks: "Land .... He surely had some he called his own," and Biggs replies "Yes ... he had some quite handsome acres."[31] The second reason was Read's desire to maintain a monopoly of trade in the area, coupled with Biggs's explanation that: "land was required to bring in colonists .... Read had it. As you know, Maoris are now reluctant to part with theirs."[32] The third reason, as Biggs says, was that Coates showed surprising initiative, was vocal, and so had to be contained: "No one would contest Coates's sly intelligence .... That made him the worse. At the slightest excuse he would go running to the law. He had a reputation for driving magistrates insane."[33] This buttresses Ihimaera's earlier comment "Ah, yes, and the Pakeha also wanted to remove all those who were troublesome" (*The Matriarch*, p. 135). Particularly disquieting to Shadbolt's Fairweather was that a man who fought for the Crown should be imprisoned and exiled without so much as a court martial: "It surely cannot be that Coates had no trial at all. He carried arms for the Queen; he at least earned a court martial."[34]

Fairweather's quibble with Biggs on points of law in respect of Te Kooti highlights Te Kooti's reluctance to submit himself to a law he was justifiably suspicious of:

> "They give offence to law and order."
> "To order, perhaps. Of law I have less competence to speak."
> "They have taken it into their own hands."
> "Which seems not unfamiliar in Poverty Bay."
> ... "The prisoners will have to be contained.
> Persuaded to give up their arms and loot."
> "And surrender themselves to colonial justice?"
> "Entirely."
> "Then you have a distinct problem, Major Biggs. Coates, in his past incarnation, has cause to believe there is none."[35]

It is in the context of the foregoing that Ihimaera's insistence on portraying a historical perspective which takes "the other side of the story" into account can be understood. He uses biblical allusions not only to foster a feeling of righteousness but also to accentuate the necessity of Te Kooti's actions. This necessity, in Ihimaera's view, is part of the chain effect of colonialism and oppression. Ihimaera's argument is that Te Kooti was persecuted, denied justice, falsely imprisoned and exiled because he was Maori, not because he had committed any crime, since no charges against him were proved (*The Matriarch*, p. 135).

Ihimaera's attempts to present a committed Maori writer's view of the Te Kooti and Matawhero issues might have sounded unconvincing but for his artful use of biblical allusions—because of their emotiveness, which he acknowledges. His intricate weaving of myth with historical fact means that *The Matriarch* does not pretend to offer an "objective" view of history as commonly understood, but a polemical counterbalance, from a Maori viewpoint, to Pakeha-biased versions. Ihimaera is aware of the polemical nature of the issues raised. David Young comments:

> Ihimaera acknowledges that his historical working in the novel will be regarded as partisan, even by many Maoris. He also admits that it contains some deliberate historical inaccuracies 'just to help maintain the fiction.' [36]

This awareness, and Ihimaera's use of the term "retaliation" as opposed to "massacre" in referring to Te Kooti's actions, among other things, exemplifies the gap between the Maori and Pakeha perspectives; for, from the massacre onwards, Shadbolt and Ihimaera part ways in their narratives.[37]

Ihimaera further confirms his intention of presenting an alternative viewpoint by mentioning the popular assumption that: "the white settlers were at prayer when the raiders made their attack on the settlement. A raid of this sort is much more indictable and much more of an atrocity if it is perpetrated before the face of God"

(*The Matriarch*, p. 159). He then systematically reconstructs the actions to contend this assumption. In Ihimaera's version, the actual killings happened on Tuesday 10 November, not on a Sunday. He asserts that, "there was no slaughter of innocents in the church at Matawhero" (*The Matriarch*, p. 160). In Ihimaera's account, the raiders only killed those who had a hand in their wrongful imprisonment (and their families), or those who were soldiers, or enemy sympathisers—Major Biggs: "Biggs, my old enemy, my nemesis ... You sent me away without trial"; J. R. Wyllie: "He was a party to my exile"; Sergeant James Padbury, who was their "guard on Wharekauri"; and Capt. James Wilson (*The Matriarch*, pp. 160–70).

The graphic details of the killing of predominantly white families during the Matawhero massacre, are there, moreover, for a purpose. Roy Murphy says of Ihimaera:

> One of his primary motives in writing *The Matriarch* was revenge on the European. He wanted to hurt the European reader .... That was why he wrote in such graphic details about the deaths of the mostly white military men and their families.[38]

This motive, he says, "stems from the predominant European view of New Zealand history." [39] And, as in most stories, the narrator's slant or perspective on the tale reflect the teller's stance or, put bluntly, what side one is on. Ihimaera's slanted comments in this vein showed the effect of criticism from Maori nationalists who during the 1980s were edging him closer towards the "radical" camp.

Assimilation or Bicultural Integration?

The tensions and conflicts, losses and changes suffered by the Maori in the nineteenth century ended in a despairing movement towards assimilation. By 1896, as Pearson states, the "Maori race was thought to be dying" and the pressure was on them to either integrate themselves into the dominant Pakeha society or become extinct.[40] Most Maori felt that there was no hope for them as a distinct people. So, through marriages and migration to the urban areas, they gradually started being assimilated. Ihimaera sees the painting of Te Rongopai—the Gospel—as an instance of early Maori attempts to integrate Pakeha and Maori values in the nineteenth century. Following the first confrontations between Maori and Pakeha, and considering that the Pakeha were by then in the majority, held the power and dictated the future, young Maori had realised even then (the late 1880s) that their future lay in an integration of both cultures. Ihimaera states that the young people "... made the house into a likeness unto themselves, the iwi, and their dreams" (*The Matriarch*, p. 185).

The painting of Te Rongopai eloquently testifies to this dream of a bicultural integration, and it is through this that Ihimaera traces and further analyses both the concept's historical origins and what they represent for the Maori. He states that while the more traditional elders felt that the young people had painted the meeting house "with little reference to tradition, an obvious break with the past", that he (Tama):

> always liked to think that the prophet would have approved, for just as he had blended the Christian faith with Maori culture to speak for the people in the new world, so also the young people attempted to show the blending of the old ways with the new and the world of the Maori in the lands of Pharaoh .... The gravity and reverence for the past were evident on all

> rafters, painted in the typical designs of the kowhaiwhai, bold red, white and black curvilinear designs .... The same reverence was also evident in the reed work .... The basic concept of the interior illustrations, whether carved, painted or woven, conformed to the outlines of tradition. But it was the filling in that was different ... unveiling the subconscious of the Maori, the persona, in highly romantic and yet realistic terms ... it was not hopelessness that the young painters showed; rather, faith ... The dream was of a new, brave, world, the new Eden where the kowhaiwhai was embellished with new colours, where painted spirals and floral patterns provided a panacea for war and a prayer for peace. It was the kind of dream that people associate with the psychedelia; it placed the Maori in the position of centrality but gave him the moko of the Pakeha. (*The Matriarch*, pp. 190–1)

Ihimaera concludes his rhapsodic description by pointing out that the human figures were "painted in the traditional style, flourishing the taiaha and mere weapons, but with blue eyes and short hair parted in the European way", exemplifying the dream of biculturalism (*The Matriarch*, p. 191).

Even then, however, he suggests, the young Maori had started feeling the tensions of their dual inheritance. Unfortunately the initial move towards integration, in Ihimaera's view, had an unpleasant tang: "Integration of people does *not* automatically make for integration of culture."[41] Ihimaera reports that the Maori were actively "encouraged to embrace Pakeha ways."[42] While doing so, "we did not really think to interpret our position in society because we were all merrily rolling downhill towards integration or assimilation, either quite sure we could retain our identity during the process or thinking to Hell with it anyway."[43] Because of this initial apathy on the part of Maori, the tendency was towards assimilation rather than bicultural integration.

Ihimaera sees the Maori as being faced with the grim realisation that their continued alienation as a people from their land, coupled with their exodus to the city, which does not have the facility nor the atmosphere for the handing-down of the culture from the elders to the younger generation, meant that their culture would die:

> Continued alienation of Maori land and of Maori people from their culture meant that the Maori was becoming landless and cultureless in his own country. As well, he was moving in greater numbers from rural areas, the earth-base of his culture, into urban areas where traditional tribal values and transmission of culture by Maori methods could not be sustained; nor were urban areas equipped then for providing for the transmission of the culture.[44]

The result was what he has come to view as a disruption of cultural continuity—a cultural faultline. This cultural dislocation was consequent on the urban "drifts", which Ihimaera believes had a common denominator—the dreams that this study has already analysed.

In the course of this analysis it has been established that Ihimaera's characterisations reflect the individual characters' level of bicultural integration, whether they reside in town or country. *The Matriarch* confirms this. There is no doubt that, to Ihimaera, Tama Mahana is truly biculturally integrated. While he is successful by Pakeha standards, he is also shown to retain his Maoritanga. He is not only married to a Pakeha, he has in fact indoctrinated his wife into knowing and accepting some basic Maori values: Regan understands, as she says, "that I didn't marry just you, I married all of you" (*The Matriarch*, p. 19). Realising what having a male issue means for Maori families, particularly to the first son of a rangatira line, she "wept when our first child, a daughter, was born. 'I am so sorry. I wanted to give you a son, so sorry,'" ater again apologises "I am so sorry, Tamatea ... that I have not given you a son" (*The Matriarch*, p. 227). It has to be understood that for Regan, brought up in a tradition that does not discriminate between male and female children, to feel as apologetic as she does about a natural phenomenon over which she has no control means only one thing—she really does appreciate Maori culture. These emotional outbursts do not suggest in the least that either Regan or Tamatea reject or neglect their daughters, for Tamatea argues for his daughters with grandfather Ihaka, reminding him: "My grandmother ... succeeded to chieftainship. And she was a woman ... Do not be dismissive about my daughters, grandfather. Or my wife" (*The Matriarch*, p. 217). Rather, both parents accept and appreciate the cultural reality. If Tamatea were a woman, it is obvious that grandfather Ihaka would have succeeded in foisting on Toroa, as heir, the leadership of the Mahana clan. Regan's understanding and appreciation of Maori ways of life, in spite of her being Pakeha, is thus ample testimony that Tamatea Mahana still retains his Maoritanga. Coupled with Tamatea's Maoritanga are his achievements in the Pakeha world: "You know how proud Mum and Dad and us kids are of you. I mean, gee, you're famous" (*The Matriarch*, p. 89).

The Matriarch illustrates the many facets of Ihimaera's theory of biculturalism, exploring its weaknesses as well as its strengths and confronting the criticisms made by opponents of the concept. It also gathers the earlier themes explored in his other writings into a larger historical pattern. The rural versus urban Maori theme becomes relevant in more than personal terms, showing the consequences of urban migration, while the group of Tama's cousins is divided into those who have attempted to make it in the Pakeha world of competitive economic enterprise and those who fall short:

> Perhaps we're too competitive and that makes us jealous of each other. But we all started off the same, surely? And we can't help it that Mum

> and Dad kept us on at school and made us get good qualifications. Our cousins had the same opportunities as us. I think you're right. We took the opportunities and they didn't. (*The Matriarch*, p. 89)

The attitudes of Tamatea's cousins, Sammy and Raina, typify the destruction of the traditional concept of family aroha in that they have come to hate Tamatea and his sister Teria for being "different". They also blame Tama and his arm of the family for depriving them of their share of "mana", in that the matriarch showered all the love on him. As Teria relates,

> [Raina] said that the reason why you've gotten on is because you were given special treatment by our grandmother .... According to Raina, our whole family has been given a head start. It has to do with the fact that Dad is the eldest son and therefore the head of the Mahana clan. And you're his eldest, and a son. The heir. (*The Matriarch*, p. 89)

Sammy confirms Raina's accusation, saying:

> You are the cause of all our troubles, Tamatea. Our Uncle Alexis, his *mate* is because of you. My sister, Raina, her sickness also. Why? Because that old lady, our grandmother, she gave you our souls, Tamatea, and left us prone to all illness. Aunt Circe tried to prevent it, but you got everything, Tamatea. Everything. (*The Matriarch*, p. 357) [Our italics]

Thus the headship of the clan, which in the cultural and traditional context functions to bring the members of the family closer to each other, becomes a reason for disharmony. Even the Maori past, the traditions and the culture are reviewed as evidence of attendant losses and a record of historical injustices :

> Then there it was, the gateway to Waituhi, the once-palisaded hill, its crumbling steps incised in dark silhouette against the sky. My heart began to swirl with the same maelstrom of past and present, of light and darkness, of elation and sadness. Every approach to Waituhi was a rebirth. At the same time it was also an acknowledgement of loss, for this was the womb of my life and it had given life to the family of the womb, generation after generation. (*The Matriarch*, p. 90)

Considered from this perspective, *The Matriarch* exposes the evolution of Ihimaera's radicalised thinking. Ihimaera uses the novel to explore and confront the historical origins of the present Maori sense of alienation and of the post-colonial tensions that still persist in this century.

A Symbol of Biculturalism

Tamatea Mahana (in *The Matriarch*) is Ihimaera's most fully developed individual character to date (except for the village of Waituhi, which is itself a character in most of Ihimaera's fiction), and so a worthy example for the analysis of Ihimaera's concept of biculturalism for Maori. Ihimaera has, in characterising him, integrated the positive values of both cultures to enable him to "bestride both worlds, to be a taniwha to both Maori and Pakeha," in the image used for the matriarch (*The Matriarch*, p. 27).

Ihimaera's constant repetition of the matriarch's "refrain" that she has made Tamatea into her own "image" and "likeness",[45] and the idea (remarked upon by C. K. Stead among others) that Tamatea's identity cannot be divorced from that of the matriarch, means that neither Tamatea nor Ihimaera's radicalised views on biculturalism which Tamatea symbolises can be adequately addressed without recourse to her.[46]

Ihimaera describes the matriarch mostly in superlatives:

> Hers is a blinding presence, imperious and commanding .... She was a most striking lady, very beautiful in a Roman sort of way .... you can glimpse just enough to realise how breathtakingly stunning she must have been. (*The Matriarch*, pp. 207–10)

Although throughout the novel she is described in lofty language and often shown to be an extraordinary woman, Tamatea's cousin, Whai, tells him that it was Wi Pere that deliberately fostered this character in her:

> But she just didn't happen to be that way. It was cultivated in her. She was made that way. She had few peers, as a Maori woman of the taniwha line, in the Maori world .... There was more—her accomplishments in the *Pakeha* world .... Your grandmother was a fine huntswoman. Well, *that* part of her life is derived directly from the Thomas Halbert line, down through Wi Pere. I suspect that Wi Pere cast his mantle on your grandmother .... Perhaps he wanted her to bestride both worlds, to be a taniwha to both Maori and Pakeha? Certainly her power, her charisma to Maori people and to Pakeha alike came from the fact that this dual training set her apart, just as it had Wi Pere himself. (*The Matriarch*, pp. 26–7)

Cousin Whai, pondering on the reasons for Wi Pere's actions, tells Tamatea: "He probably wanted to make her into a likeness. Like himself."[47] This explains the matriarch's obsession with this phrase which she uses many times in respect of Tamatea, and her insistence that Tamatea learn all the basic rules and skills of both Maori and Pakeha ways of fighting. She tells Tamatea:

> One day, e mokopuna, this will be your task. You must grasp the tools of the Pakeha and understand them. Particularly, you must understand

> the words of the white man, not only what he says but what he really means. (*The Matriarch*, p. 230)

And later still the matriarch, in dedicating Tamatea to what she perceives as his destiny—to fight to regain and secure the land for the people—tells him:

> I have taught you to be a Maori and to fight in a Maori way. But there is another lesson which you must learn, one which my own great-uncle taught me when I was a child. He sent me away from this place to another across the sea. I did not understand then, but I did when I returned .... I have taught you how to fight the Pakeha. But I had forgotten that to fight the Pakeha you must learn to be like him. You must become a Pakeha, think like him, act like him and, when you know you are in his image then turn your knowledge to his destruction. (*The Matriarch*, p. 427)

It is probably in the *nga pungawerewere* (spider) scene that Ihimaera best dramatises the potency of some of the powers with which the matriarch had infused Tamatea, powers which he was later to demonstrate in the succession fight with Toroa for the leadership of the Mahana clan. But the spider scene, apart from any other associations, serves to establish the fact that Tamatea, in inheriting the matriarch's mantle, has also inherited some of her awesome powers for, as he relates;

> there is no doubt that the matriarch called to Uncle Manaaki and Hiraina, *guard the child* (and years later, I called in the same fashion to my daughter, Miranda, and she appeared beside me saying, 'Yes, Daddy? You wanted me?') (*The Matriarch*, p. 289)

In spite of Tamatea's symbolic representation of Ihimaera's concept of biculturalism, it is apparent that the author's characterisation of the matriarch, imbuing her with such domineering and larger-than-life characteristics, stunts some aspects of Tamatea's development as a character. Yet given the impression which the title and the matriarch's dominance of the novel creates, some critics, amongst them Janet Potiki and Atareta Poananga, have expressed reservations about how realistic Ihimaera's characterisation of the matriarch is. Janet Potiki writes:

> Though a woman is at the centre of the book, and others are included, I felt lonely for any sense of companionship among women. Tiana, Artemis and the mythical Hine Te Ariki join in times of extreme danger, but in day-to-day life warm, shared relationships between women are missing.[48]

It is probably this lack of warmth in the female characters, particularly Tiana, and Ihimaera's insistence on the *noa* nature of women in respect of certain Maori ceremonies that has led Atareta Poananga absurdly to see the novel as a "profoundly woman-hating book."[49] Elizabeth Caffin holds a different view of the matriarch's character: "As a tyrant within the family, shaping her relatives to her will, and as a woman of stature on the marae, she is entirely convincing."[50] The matriarch is individually convincing in spite of what Caffin sees as her representative role in expressing "Maori anger at the pillage and destruction by the Pakeha, at the loss of land and mana";[51] and in embodying Ihimaera's radicalised concept of biculturalism. As Potiki remarks, there are conflicts within her that give her strength as a person and as a character:

> A warrior since birth, she must retain what is Maori and reconcile with this those Pakeha things that have become part of herself. The weight of both cultures is in force against her and she strives to retain the balance, the mana Maori that asserts Maori as equal to Pakeha.[52]

Ihimaera believes that this balance, this strength, is consistently becoming more difficult for her to retain. As the matriarch symbolised a synthesis of Te Kooti as her darker side and Wi Pere as her lighter side, so does Tamatea Mahana. (*The Matriarch*, p. 294) All her dedication and teaching have been aimed towards Tamatea accomplishing what the matriarch had realised was beyond her to do—a unification of both forces, the darker and the lighter, a merger of both cultures, Maori and Pakeha. Ihimaera's extensive use of Wi Pere's parliamentary debates and the comments that Wi Pere chose Artemis "to carry on his fight" support the bicultural argument in a vicarious way (*The Matriarch*, p. 346). Wi Pere's arguments are demonstrably for solutions to the issues of land sales that would neither "estrange the two races" nor stir up "fighting between them" (*The Matriarch*, pp. 336–7). This is consistent in some aspects with the matriarch's, and Ihimaera's, views on the issue. But its significance lies in Ihimaera's identifying with Wi Pere because he, as Ihimaera argues, attempted to effect and fight for change, and for bicultural integration from within the system: "He has said publicly he identifies with Wi Pere for he worked from *within* to make change."[53]

Ihimaera's characterisation of Tamatea Mahana reflects the author's continuing ambivalence about the concept of biculturalism, in the face of the slow pace of change, and of the body of opinion that sees biculturalism as little better than assimilation. Ihimaera's views on the concept have progressed beyond seeing it as merely an integration of Maori and Pakeha cultural values, to seeing it embracing the economic and social realities of existence. Tamatea demonstrates an awareness of all the dialectics of biculturalism—cultural, social, and economic.

The fact that Tamatea inherited Artemis's mantle and its attendant powers testifies to his mana; his mana and Maoritanga are not only intact, but augmented by the restraint of the Pakeha cultural values which he has imbibed. This is exemplified by the long drawn out "heir crisis", instigated by grandfather Ihaka. The five years of festering conflict culminates in the duel on the marae, and Tamatea has to call, not on his Pakeha heritage and learning (in law), but on the very depth of his Maori teachings:

> I was being faced by the most important test of my life. I was contesting my grandfather and his whangai for my mana. By doing this publicly all of us risked everything; the winner would take all .... Despite my objections, Ihaka would not waive his purpose ... I stood up. I put both my hands into the air and began to squeeze. Toroa started to gasp, to fight against an invisible presence. I squeezed even tighter and he was forced to the ground .... Bewildered, Ihaka tried to support him. Then he knew. He looked across at me in fear .... Enough, Tamatea! Tiana said ... I stopped and Toroa reeled from my grasp. (*The Matriarch*, pp. 400–2)

Arguably, Ihimaera lauds Tamatea's possession of the positive qualities of the matriarch as much as he criticises his evident possession of the destructive ones, but this is a reflection of the author's ambivalence which has already been noted. But the narrative, while not highlighting Tamatea's engaging in "wars" with the Pakeha as the matriarch intends, provides Ihimaera with the avenue to explore those specifics that he believes are obstacles to biculturalism. Chief amongst these obstacles is the concept of separatism which has been mentioned with respect to Api in both "Clenched Fist" and "Tent on the Home Ground", but which will also be discussed in the next chaper under thc hcading "The Dilemma".

As has been highlighted in the course of this analysis, critics of Ihimaera's concept of biculturalism, particularly the Maori "nationalists" , believe that, essentially, there is no distinction between the early dream of assimilation and the later dream of biculturalism. Atareta Poananga asserts in the passage quoted earlier:

> Today a new Pakeha co-optive strategy is coined—biculturalism—assimilation in another guise,

> because the outcome is the same .... You see there is only one destiny—to be white, to succeed in white things.[54]

It is on the basis of this assertion that there has been a concerted assault on the concept of biculturalism. The way Maori nationalists see the reality of their situation in New Zealand has led both to a shattering of the dreams already analysed, and to Ihimaera's ambivalence and his radicalised views in *The Matriarch*.

4

♥♠♥

Myth and Modern Reality: the Dilemma of Biculturalism in Ihimaera's Recent Fiction

Ihimaera's Recent Fiction: *The Whale Rider*

Richard Corballis and Simon Garrett, remarking on the allegorical nature of Ihimaera's short story "The Whale" in *Pounamu, Pounamu*, and the whale's powerful symbolism, also describe Ihimaera's personification of the waning Maoritanga in the form of the dying kaumatua, who embodies "the traditional Maori ways."[1] They see the two forms of symbolism combined in the whale: "The old man has become the dying whale."[2] The fleeing gulls in Ihimaera's story clutch "in their claws", not the whale's flesh which they have been stripping, but the old man's "shouted words". The author has further extended the allegory, they suggest, to equate both the dying whale and the stranded Kaumatua with the declining Maoritanga.

The Whale Rider evokes this image, but with a significant qualification. In "The Whale" the kaumatua did not see any hope for Maoritanga, since the only grandchild that had shown any enthusiasm for it had turned her back on both the old man's teachings and the Maori world, in the belief that neither could equip her to cope with the Pakeha world in which she has to live. In *The Whale Rider*, on the other hand, Ihimaera is more hopeful. He sees the fate of the Maori as inextricably entwined with the "fate of the sea's denizens" symbolised by the whale; for as Koro Apirana[3] pointedly says:

> The whale is a sign .... It has stranded itself here. If we are able to return it to the sea, then that will be proof that the oneness is still with us. If we are not able to return it, then this is because we have become weak. If it lives, we live. If it dies, we die. Not only its salvation but ours is waiting out there. (*The Whale Rider*, p. 96)

As in his earlier works, Ihimaera in *The Whale Rider* covers a wide range of themes. Some he has already explored; but some old themes are modified. Such issues as urban migration and its attendant problems for urban Maori are viewed through the travels and experiences of Rawiri. Faced with the reality of urban existence in a modern economy, and without skills, some of the young Maori in urban centres have made dramatic changes,

> ... to themselves or their lives .... In the search for fame, fortune, power and success, some of my cousins had opted for the base metal and not the gold. They may have turned their lives upside down in the process, like Sydney Bridge's reflection in the harbour, but they always craved the respect of our whanau. (*The Whale Rider*, pp. 51–2)

Ihimaera writes that such characters become reluctant for their whanau to see or know how they live:

> But always, in the early morning, when the sunlight was beginning to crack the midnight glamour, the memories would come seeping through. 'How's our Nanny? How's our Koro? If you write to them, don't tell them that you saw us like *this*' ... They weren't embarrassed, but hiding the way they lived was one way of maintaining the respect. (*The Whale Rider*, pp. 51–2)

Ihimaera highlights such issues as Maoritanga and Maori nationalism through Koro Apirana's wananga sessions from which he hoped to "pass on the knowledge, the sacred kumara" to the younger generation (*The Whale Rider*, p. 59). This and his other efforts are made to ensure that while the people are being "prepared ... to cope with the new challenges and the new technology", they will still be Maori (*The Whale Rider*, pp. 58–9). Ihimaera in *The Whale Rider* also vicariously confronts such other issues as racism, for instance, in describing the experiences in Australia and Papua New Guinea through which Rawiri states that he "grew into an understanding of [himself] as a Maori" (*The Whale Rider*, p. 57). Clara's blatant racism, likening Rawiri to a stray dog which her son has brought home, and her comment at the accident in which Bernard is killed that: "It's only a native", lead Rawiri to reflect sadly on Jeff's own reactions:

> 'I don't blame you,' I said to Jeff. 'You can't help being who you are' .... [and I felt] sadness that a friend I thought I had would so automatically react to the assumptions of his culture. *And would I be next?* (*The Whale Rider*, p. 61)

But it is through the exposition of the traditional concepts of conservation of nature and respect for the stranded whales that Ihimaera develops his call for a heightened sensitivity to the Maori's avowed affinity with nature. Richard Corballis and Simon Garrett in their explanatory note on stranded whales in "The Whale" say: "In Maori folk-lore beached whales generally signify an abundance of food."[4] Ihimaera confirms this view, stating that "in Maori terms a stranded whale was traditionally a gift from the Gods" (*The Whale Rider*, p. 84). But Koro Apirana views the massive destruction and wastage of nature's resources signified by the beaching of two hundred whales as being consequent on man's transgressions of his pact with nature: "But we have not always kept our pact with Tangaroa, and in these days of commercialism it is not always easy to resist temptation" (*The Whale Rider*, p. 41). Koro Apirana's argument stems from Ihimaera's claims, mentioned earlier, of a living relationship and affinity between the Maori and the land, the elements, and nature. This is an aspect of Maoritanga which he believes is being eroded within the new social structure and the urban environment. In Ihimaera's writings, one of the effects of the coming of the Pakeha, he says, is that the Maori have lost touch with the natural forces with which they were meant to be in harmony. Koro Apirana's *karakia* and *korero* explicates this point:

> Once, our world was one where the Gods talked to our ancestors and man talked with the Gods. Sometimes the Gods gave our ancestors special powers. For instance, our ancestor Paikea ... was given power to talk to whales and to command them. In this way, man, tipua and Gods lived in close communion with one another. (*The Whale Rider*, p. 95)

Ihimaera relates:

> He came riding through the sea, our sea god Kahutia Te Rangi, astride his tipua, and he brought with him the mauri, the life-giving forces which would enable us to live in close communion with the world .... They were very special because among other things, they gave instructions on how man might korero with the beasts and creatures of the sea so that all could live in helpful partnership. They taught *oneness*. (*The Whale Rider*, p. 27)

In *The Matriarch*, both Tamatea (tutored by the matriarch) and the matriarch herself had learnt how to harness some of these natural forces for specific purposes. Although some of the uses are destructive, as shown in the *nga pungawerewere* episode at the hui in Wellington and Tamatea's fight with Toroa on the marae, they are, however, evidence of the potency of the forces which were available to Maori when they were close to nature.[5] Ihimaera argues that this is an aspect of the culture that cannot be sustained in the urban centres.

In a 1984 essay, "Environment, Security and Identity: a 'Maui-esque' viewpoint", Ihimaera shows some modern responses to such Maori claims and beliefs as the following:

> For Maori people the environment has been, and still continues to be, living, breathing and possessing a life force. ... At birth, for instance, the afterbirth of a child was buried in the earth not only to bind the child with the earth but also to reinforce, in a psychical manner, his or her relationship with a particular hearth—the marae or turangawaewae.[6]

Ihimaera and Piddington say that "in most cases, whenever this concept of a living relationship between the Maori and his environment is mentioned", one of the reactions of the audience "is to dismiss the concept as being unsophisticated, rather romantic but irrelevant."[7] Koro Apirana, in *The Whale Rider*, blames this rejection on man's arrogance, and his compartmentalising of nature and the world into:

> that half he could believe in and that half he could not believe in. The real and the unreal. The natural and supernatural .... The scientific and the fantastic. He put a barrier between both worlds and everything on his side was called rational and everything on the other side was called irrational. Belief in our *Maori Gods*, he emphasised, has often been considered irrational. (*The Whale Rider*, p. 96)

This response, Ihimaera argues, is fostered by the cultural dislocation which is a consequence of urban migration. He repeatedly makes the point that these migrations "drove the wedge between the old and the new"; emphasising the difficulty of urbanised Maori imbibing the traditional concepts, the traditional world view (*The Matriarch*, p. 232). In *The Whale Rider*, however, he urges the reestablishment of this rapport and communion with nature, arguing as Koro Apirana does, that "if we have forgotten the communion then we have ceased to be Maori" (*The Whale Rider*, p. 96). In *The Whale Rider* he also seeks to express the similarity and relevance of some of these Maori traditional beliefs and world views to those of contemporary society. The notion of respect for and preservation of animal life is seen, for instance, as analogous to the current wave of interest in nature conservation: "We try never to overfish for to do so would be to take greedy advantage of Tangaroa and would bring retribution" (*The Whale Rider*, p. 40).

The Whale Rider fulfils two other basic functions apart from the re-affirmation of the fundamental principles of the concept of biculturalism. It is a feminist restatement, a recanting, of some of the views expressed in Ihimaera's earlier writings: views on women in Maori traditional societies and on the marae, issues of leadership, and the laws of tapu, which were strongly expressed in *The Matriarch*, and for which critics such as Atareta Poananga erroneously characterised that novel as biased and "woman-hating".[8]

Ihimaera states that "by Maori custom, leadership was hereditary and normally the mantle of mana fell from the eldest son to the eldest son" (*The Whale Rider*, p. 14); and that: "The active leadership of the tribe, the iwi, was generally a male prerogative" (*The Matriarch*, p. 207). The Maori proverb which some elders use to reprimand the matriarch, saying: "[Her] neck should be wrung because it is only the rooster which crows", also reflects this custom (*The Matriarch*, p. 112). But despite these assertions, the custom, as exemplified by the matriarch herself, makes allowances for circumstances where the first-born is female:

> Sometimes, however, it happened that the first-born of the senior rangatira line was not a male but rather a woman. She was then made a priestess and accorded the greatest respect as a wahine ariki .... The East Coast tribes revered such high born women and allowed them to speak in council on the marae .... The

> matriarch was one such woman, a wahine ariki. (*The Matriarch*, pp. 208)

I believe that Atareta Poananga's absurdly emotive criticism ignores the facts of the tradition, and is an undue extension of feminist criticism.

In *The Whale Rider*, Ihimaera specifically restates the idea of male dominance on the marae which is a central focus of some of the conflicts in *The Matriarch*, but he gives it a dramatic twist:

> She was a big chief, descended as she was from Apanui, after whom Nanny's tribe was named. The story we liked best was the one telling how Mihi had stood on a marae at Rotorua. "Sit down," a chief had yelled, enraged. "Sit down," because women weren't supposed to stand up and speak on the marae. But Mihi had replied, "No *you* sit down! I am a senior line to yours!" Not only that, but Mihi had then turned her back to him, bent over, lifted up her petticoats and said, "Anyway, here is the place where you come from!" In this way Mihi had emphasised that all men are born of women. (*The Whale Rider*, p. 66)

Although Mihi encounters similar attitudes to those encountered by the matriarch from the men on the marae, she does not engage in protracted squabbles for ascendancy or even the right to speak; rather, she silences her detractors with a single action of irrefutable and effective "logic". Women do, indeed, precede men.

In *The Whale Rider* Ihimaera also tells the story of Muriwai, Nanny Flowers's famous ancestor, in the context of criticism that "Nanny Flowers was always 'stepping out of line' ". It was a noble thing that Muriwai did—if 'out of line', then laudably so; her declaration, "Now I shall make myself a man", shows her assumption of the powers and the tapu that traditionally accompany tasks such as she was undertaking—to save the Maataatua canoe:

> "If Muriwai hadn't done that," Nanny used to say, "the canoe would have been wrecked." Then she would hold up her arms and say, "And I am proud that Muriwai's blood flows in my veins." (*The Whale Rider*, p. 17)

The Whale Rider is dedicated to "Jessica Kiri and Olivia Ata, [Ihimaera's two daughters] the best girls in the whole wide world"; one cannot help but notice the similar expression which has Koro Apirana recanting his earlier views about the leadership capacity of women and declaring to Kahu, whom he has consistently rejected because she is female: "You're the best mokopuna in the whole wide world ... Boy or girl, it doesn't matter" (*The Whale Rider*, p. 121). Ihimaera states in *The Whale Rider* not only that: "Girls can do anything these days", but that often they can do better than boys, as is exemplified by Kahu's success in bringing the stone from the depth of the ocean where all the boys had failed (*The Whale Rider*, pp. 65, 74–5). According to Kai Karanga, the female whale, "it takes the males longer than the females to understand" (*The Whale Rider*, p. 115).

But above all else, *The Whale Rider* is an affirmation of hope in the survival of the Maori race, which is signified by Kahu's success in saving the stranded whales, recalling Koro Apirana's earlier comment that the Maori fate was inextricably entwined with that of the stranded whales. It also reviews biculturalism from a feminist viewpoint, acknowledging that in these troubled times, the salvation of the world of the Maori lies in the hands of Kahu and other women, as the last wooden spear that Paikea had thrown, saying:

> "Let this one be planted in the years to come when the people are troubled and the mauri is most needed." And the mauri, [talisman] soaring through the sky came to rest in the earth where the after-birth of a female child would be placed. (*The Whale Rider*, p. 115)

While it is not the intention of this analysis to assess the influences of criticism on Ihimaera's writings in general, it is obvious that some of these criticisms are affecting the consistency of his views, especially as they relate to his concept of biculturalism, but also as they relate to contemporary versus traditional values.

The Dilemma of Biculturalism

While Ihimaera's later writings present a reality for the Maori which is contrary to the dreams reviewed in his earlier writings, they particularly accentuate a dilemma inherent in the concept of biculturalism for Maori. The reality of attempts at biculturalism, as evinced in his writings, is a state of tension consequent on the dispossession of land, urban drift, frustrated hopes, racism, and social injustice, which eventuates in only a minority of Maori making it in the Pakeha world:

> We are Maori. We are Polynesian. We inhabit a minority space within a majority framework. We are the unemployed, the social time bomb. About eighty per cent of us live in city areas. Half of us are under the age of 19 and without skills in our culture. Our world is beset with pressures from within and without .... We are the dispossessed, the under-educated .... We are one in four children who appear before the Children's Court .... This is the bleak scenario.[9]

The dilemma, which is inherent in Ihimaera's concept of biculturalism, is how to reconcile Maori traditional values and demands with a modern, and very competitive, social system. Ihimaera recognises the stifling effect of some of these demands and obligations on young Maori as they try to find their feet in the new world, particularly the insensitivity of the elders to the constraints of the new social structure, where time is of the utmost importance, and in which one does not leave one's work or means of livelihood at whim:

> I had just sneaked into work, late again as usual, when the phone rang at my desk.
>
> —Hullo? I answered.
>
> There was a click at the other end and muffled mutterings of the caller as she tried to answer me.
>
> —Hullo? she called. Anybody there? Aue, damn phone!
>
> —Auntie? Auntie Hiraina? I guessed.
>
> I heard a long sigh of relief.
>
> —I been trying to reach you for ages, Auntie said. Ever since the plane got in at Wellington.
>
> —What the heck are you doing down here!
>
> —I'm waiting for you, Tama. Can you come and pick me up?
>
> —Oh Auntie . . .
>
> —Never mind about work. This is important. I've come to collect our patu pounamu . . . (*The New Net Goes Fishing*, p. 107)

While Maori are in a rural setting, their culture deems it appropriate, and indeed socialises the young, to be at the beck and call of their elders. This response is neither practicable nor desirable in the new social structure. Yet Ihimaera has told John Beston that he believes that some of these cultural and social values should not be allowed to perish, saying: "I hope that I can encourage Maori people to resist further change in the villages."[10] This paradox accounts for some of the stresses in his fiction. It is, however, on the basis of the traditional family concept already discussed that an issue such as the one raised by Ihimaera in *Whanau*—of what to do with an aged kaumatua—becomes relevant and poignant. Does one follow the Pakeha solution of confining him to a home, where he will get excellent medical care, but probably die of loneliness in the cold anonymity of such a place?

> After what Doctor Park told me about his condition, I feel worried. Annie shouldn't have taken

> him from the hospital. And as for my putting him in a home, I wasn't doing that to get rid of him! .... I wanted him to receive proper medical attention. I was doing it for Dad. (*Whanau*, p. 126)

Or does one keep him amongst his people where he, again, probably would die, but where he would be happy among the family, surrounded by aroha and warmth:

> Oh, David, I thought that Annie could, just probably, be right about Dad. That being in a hospital would not be as good for him as recuperating in the village, among the people who mattered most to him. That if there was no hope of his getting better, then he should live his remaining days in the place where he'd been born. And then, I saw what my actions must look like from Annie's point of view. ... It's just that my people value their old ones so highly that they feel disgust for anyone who would do that to their father. They hate me because I would do that not only to my father but to their kaumatua. (*Whanau*, p. 127)

This sort of dilemma, as Alistair Fox notes, is a "powerful dramatization of the problems facing the new [Maori] generation in its attempts to find a relation between two worlds with ostensibly opposed sets of values."[11]

Ihimaera's fiction also establishes a link between urban drift, the individualism and anonymity of city life, and the reality of the high incidence of crimes involving Maori. In his view, the total lack of the traditional mechanism of censure in the urban environment, as mentioned, results in Maori throwing caution to the wind. They often do what they would not dare to do in the village, because there is no one to censure their actions.

Ihimaera's analysis of who is to blame on issues of social injustice, racism, and frustrated hopes and ambitions, exposes the dilemma of biculturalism; it also reveals a deep frustration at the slow pace of change. While he accepts the practicality of the Pakeha social structure which encourages individuals to be responsible for their fate, and exhorts Maori to overcome their reticence and integrate themselves into the larger society, he also holds this society culpable for creating an atmosphere that disadvantages the Maori, even before the race is started.

Ihimaera feels that some Pakeha attitudes to Maori accentuate the disadvantages already inherent in the social and cultural differences between the two races. He shows this through the comments and actions of characters such as the man in "The Escalator" who tells Miriama that the stairs, not the escalator, are meant for people like her. Or the woman in "A Sense of Belonging" who refuses to be served by the teller, Pari Wharepapa, because she is Maori. Even through the university lecturer who, "pointing out a typically Maori home", tells his class "with a sneer" that: "No matter what opportunities one gives Maoris, one will always find them in homes like these" (*The Matriarch*, p. 105). The resolution of some of these episodes shows an awareness that these attitudes and actions are not condoned by all: witness the encouragements of the shop attendant to Miriama in "The Escalator" and by Mr Morley, the bank manager, in the case of Pari Wharepapa in "A Sense of Belonging". But they also throw Ihimaera's dilemma into broad relief, showing why he cautions that it is hard to know when a slight or discourtesy is meant or implied: "In New Zealand Pakeha-Maori relations aren't black and white, they're gray, or brown-white. It's difficult to say when hurt is intended or imagined, or when there's discrimination."[12]

Ihimaera gives the reasons for his initial restraint and disinclination to take potshots indiscriminately at the Pakeha as stemming from his "having a foot in both Maori and Pakeha camps."[13] He sees his role as that of fostering the spirit of "te manaaki—mutual respect, mutual aroha among Maori and Pakeha for each other's cultural values and attitudes."[14] In his view, an ability to bestride both worlds is an essential quality for this role. Ihimaera sees himself as ideally suited for the role, not only because he has been married to a Pakeha, and so personally embodies, in his life and in his children, the idea of biculturalism which he advocates, but also because he is trusted and respected by both Maori and Pakeha.

As the first Maori novelist to be published, Ihimaera has presented the Maori side of the story and has opened the door for other Maori to follow suit. This act alone has ensured a place and high mana for him in Maori thinking— even among his detractors:

> Witi Ihimaera, the author, has become a legendary figure among the Pakeha literary establishment, one of the first school of Maori writers to appear in the 1970s. He is now firmly entrenched as one of the leading Maori writers— [and has a] reputation assured even if he never writes again. [15]

Also, his posting as New Zealand Consul in New York, a responsibility that recognised his talent and ability to represent New Zealand on the international scene, was indicative of his high standing among the Pakeha. In close combination, both these vocations, that of writer and that of diplomat, have amply endowed him with the qualities necessary to mediate between the Maori and Pakeha. This includes an ability to be heard by both parties; and this is where his writings are invaluable. Atareta Poananga describes Ihimaera as having "an engaging, charming, open, disarming personality, embracing of both Pakeha and Maori, thoroughly bicultural in Pakeha eyes but without a trace of hostility to the Pakeha and their ways .... He is a Maori Pakeha can feel comfortable with, for unlike Maori "radicals" and "separatists" he is easy to be with, nonchallenging, non-threatening and undemanding."[16] In spite of the apparent sarcasm and criticism directed at Ihimaera by Atareta Poananga in her essay, the kernel of her assessment is correct, and the qualities she identifies are essentially those that equip Ihimaera ideally for the role of mediator.

Viewed from the above perspective, and considered alongside his own argument for a broader application of biculturalism, Ihimaera's new stance and radicalised viewpoint (which urges the necessity of separatist programmes to ensure the survival of Maori culture) becomes paradoxical: "... to achieve these things may require what look like 'separate' institutions or separate programmes of support."[17] Ihimaera himself recognises the validity of some of the arguments that have led to concerted assaults on the concept of biculturalism by Maori activists; and advocates: "some separate development" as "necessary to the alteration of our direction as a nation."[18] Even his comment "that the Maori cultural base needed to be regained if the Maori was not to become simply a brown Pakeha",[19] pre-figures the stance of members of Te Ahi Kaa, Keepers of the Fire:

> We are not anti-white. We are pro-Maori. So many of our people are told in so many ways every day that it is not good to be Maori. We want to rebuild the sense of pride in the Maori identity ... so that our people will take that identity with them and wear it proudly and consciously where ever they are—at home, at work, on the marae, in the institutions where they work.[20]

Critics of biculturalism, such as Maori nationalists represented by Te Ahi Kaa, argue that the Pakeha does not want Maori in positions of power; nor do they want to share power with Maori. This parallels Ihimaera's comment that: "The Pakeha do not want the Maori to be equal" (*The Matriarch*, p. 50). Ihimaera seems to buy their argument that separatism would enhance the survival of Maori culture, but he also believes that on attainment of "equality" and "establishment of symbols of culture", both Maori and Pakeha would then be able to hold such symbols in common.[21] Sceptics of both races would find this theory impracticable, but what is most pertinent is that it has created a dilemma for this proponent of the concept of biculturalism. It is hard to reconcile his views on racial harmony with the divisive arguments of Maori activists who are opting for separatism — a stance he now supports; it is also hard to promote the idea of "equality" in a dual culture while being aware that the number of New Zealanders, Maori or Pakeha, who share his ideal may be few.

This analysis has striven to plot Ihimaera's definition, development, and application of the concept of biculturalism as a response to the Maori sense of post-colonial tension and alienation. In the process it has noted the often subtle shifts and changes of emphasis with regard to the concept, which are indicative of Ihimaera's changing attitude towards the Pakeha, and his vacillations in the face of concerted criticism from Maori activists. The change of tack is not suprising, given Ihimaera's stated aim of becoming a writer who can present the Maori side of the story from a Maori perspective. It thus stands to reason that he should listen to "the voices" of the people whom he believes that he represents: "... he has always been conscious of pressure from the past—voices chanting in the dark and saying, Yes that's right, No that's wrong."[22]

While Ihimaera the diplomat has been a mouthpiece for all New Zealanders, Ihimaera the writer sees himself as a mouthpiece for Maori people. As he says, it is "apparent that I have been sometimes a writer, something *more* of a Maori", and this dual role has its resultant paradoxes which are made more complex by Maori activists with their strident demands for separatism.[23]

It has been noted that Ihimaera's social consciousness and socialisation presuppose that he should articulate Maori concerns and grievances while at the same time remaining accountable to Maoridom for his utterances. This has led, in some instances, to Ihimaera's later writings restating, modifying, or refuting views already expressed in his earlier works. This analysis has already shown the restatements in *The New Net Goes Fishing* and *The Matriarch* of views contained in *Pounamu, Pounamu*, *Tangi* and to some extent *Whanau*, which Ihimaera felt no longer reflected current realities of the Maori. The same is true of

The Whale Rider, which restates concepts already covered by his earlier writings, but with an added feminist variant.

However, underlying all the views, and subtle shifts, Ihimaera's faith in biculturalism as a structured form of adaptation and a viable Maori stand against the possibility of total assimilation, or cultural annihilation, remains strong. Ihimaera sees it as the only logical answer to Koro Apirana's vital questions: "Will we have prepared the [Maori] people to cope with the new challenges and the new technology? And will they still be Maori?" (*The Whale Rider*, p. 59). Even his admission that "our journey was possibly more difficult because it had to be undertaken within Pakeha terms of acceptability" is basically an acknowledgement of social reality: "We were a minority and much of our progress was dependent on Pakeha goodwill" (*The Whale Rider*, p. 57). The reality Ihimaera acknowledges is that New Zealand now belongs to both races, Maori and Pakeha, with the Pakeha comprising the majority, and that within this framework both races have to work together for the good of all.

5

Conclusion

When one considers the historical context from which Ihimaera is writing—a white settler society in which European migrants outnumber the indigenous people by an overwhelming majority—the depth of the social realism and the broad, inclusive vision of his writings assume significance. Of particular relevance are his views on the role of the imaginative writer in contemporary society, which are similar in many respects to those expressed by other indigenous writers such as Achebe and Ngugi Wa Thiong'o, among others. Ihimaera declares that his aim in writing is didactic: to teach young urbanised Maori about the Maori aspect of their dual heritage: "My first priority is to the young Maori, the ones who have suffered most with the erosion of the Maori map, the ones who are Maori by colour but who have no emotional identity as Maori."[1] In an interview with John B. Beston Ihimaera says of his first book: "I wanted *Pounamu, Pounamu* to go into the schools, into English classes, because it would reach both Maori and Pakeha kids of age fourteen - fifteen or higher. I wanted it to help other Maoris especially."[2] Ihimaera also believes that *Pounamu, Pounamu* has "given Maori kids an idea of what it's like to be Maori, the emotional experience."[3]

In the context of the intense individualism which Ihimaera believes is the hallmark of European culture, he has always promoted Maoritanga as an identity based on communally-held values. His call for a revaluation of things Maori requires—for Pakeha and Maori—a learning re-learning about the traditions which uphold these values. Ihimaera has had, like other writers, to recreate his society's historical past to counter earlier assumptions that the Maori did not have any history or culture. He repeatedly tells this simple story, for instance:

> Ask who discovered New Zealand and you will be told Abel Tasman. But the answer, as given by Maori history, is Kupe. And that, quite simply, is why I began to write. To make New Zealanders aware of their 'other,' Maori, heritage.[4]

So in his early writing he assiduously cultivated and developed themes that highlighted the indigenous culture and traditions of his society, both for the enlightenment of culturally alienated Maori, as he says, and of the larger New Zealand society—leading to the charge of pastoralism and romanticism which critics such as Simms and Arvidson have labelled him with. But his recent writings have shown a shift in emphasis. They manifest a pronounced anger at the slow pace of change, leading to a more radical and militant literature.

The hiatus in Ihimaera's writing career, as already outlined, was a deliberate decision to stop and revaluate his social consciousness in the light of prevailing social, economic and political circumstances affecting the Maori people at the time. It led to his developing a more radical and sharpened awareness of Maori post-colonial tensions and "the reality of the times" as he perceived them:

> The reality of 1975 was a hardening of attitudes on both sides. Of inflexibility. Of infighting. By 1975 I felt my vision was out of date and, tragically, so encompassing and so established that it wasn't leaving room enough for the new reality to punch through. I made a conscious decision to stop writing.[5]

Ihimaera believed that what was needed was a literature that could reach "across the empty spaces" and make the connection "between Maori and Pakeha in a more hard-hitting and realistic fashion."[6] *The Matriarch* and, to a lesser extent, *The Whale Rider*, were designed to do just that.

It is my belief that Ihimaera has reduced the feat of Colossus to mundane levels by insisting that bestriding both worlds — Maori and Pakeha — is the entitlement of all New Zealanders, and that biculturalism is an ideal that all can and should strive for; that, particularly for Pakeha New Zealanders, occasionally dipping their beak into the spring of Maoriness — tokenism — is not enough. On the other hand, he has found that nothing is quite "enough", either, for critics of biculturalism from the Maori side. It is perhaps not surprising, given Ihimaera's sensitivity to Maori concerns, that he perceives the criticisms of such Maori nationalists as Atareta Poananga as questioning his commitment to Maori issues. It is for this reason that he has occasionally felt the need, unnecessarily I believe, to justify his position, action, fiction, or the use to which he puts materials in his writings. Cousin Whai, in *The Matriarch*, paints a lively portrait of his most serious critic:

> And there's Atareta — the same thing, a brilliant degree in Political Science in Auckland, her father was with the UN Force in the Middle East, now she is with Foreign Affairs, looking like a Parisian model — she is probably more of a radical than Donna [Awatere] is. She smoulders. Nobody can dampen her firc, her passion .... In fact, these days, you look around and, huh, it seems as if all our men have gone soft. The women seem to be doing most of the protesting and jumping up and down these days. Certainly they are the ones who are taking Maori issues to the extremities of action. (*The Matriarch*, p. 25)

Ihimaera's high regard for Atareta Poananga is evident. Poananga, however, believes that Ihimaera, by not coming to her defence when she had problems with their employer, the Ministry of Foreign Affairs, had betrayed the bonds of both *manaakitanga* and *whanuangatanga*, as one Maori to another. In an interview with Nicola Legat, she has stated:

> Witi and I were called up. He was told he could be fired too because he had also gone public .... Later he crumbled under the pressure. A year later he signed an affidavit against me .... When it comes to the crunch a lot of our men opt out. That's a lesson I've learned.[7]

Nicola Legat goes further to say of Atareta Poananga that: "There is a clear sense that she feels Ihimaera's action as a betrayal."[8]

Nevertheless, this study has shown that Ihimaera has been responding to such criticisms as Poananga's. His latest fiction, *The Whale Rider*, as already highlighted, shows a feminist bias that reflects Ihimaera's accommodation of the criticism that *The Matriarch* is a misogynist work. Also, Ihimaera apparently agreed with Roy Murphy that "One of his [Ihimaera's] primary motives in writing *The Matriarch* was revenge on the European", and he has said openly: "If you want them to hurt, you don't write about the massacre of Maori people, you write about the massacre of European people, ... My business is to make European people cry."[9] These attitudes seem to stem from Ihimaera's desire to portray the image of a committed Maori writer.

Ihimaera's critical analysis both of the Maori sense of alienation, and of the political and social injustices inflicted on the Maori by the Pakeha, are adequately portrayed in his writings. Such Pakeha-alienating comments as the above are unnecessary as an explication of his motives; rather, they seem aimed at refuting the accusation that he is not political enough or committed enough to Maori issues and to redressing Maori grievances. More importantly, such comments seem inconsistent with his concept of biculturalism, given his admission that "our journey was possibly more difficult because it had to be undertaken within Pakeha terms of acceptability"; that Maori "were a minority" within the framework of majority Pakeha domination, and much of their "progress was dependent on Pakeha goodwill"

(*The Whale Rider*, p. 57). Such inconsistencies could lead to the compromising of Ihimaera's integrity if his views are perceived to be easily influenced by critics; neither the exhibition of a Mongrel Mob patch, nor vociferous radicalism, constitute the qualities of Maori-ness.

Given all the arguments for and against the concepts of biculturalism and separatism which Ihimaera's writings have revealed, they do demonstrate that he still sees the concept of biculturalism, as he defines it, as the most practicable and desirable end, and in the long-run most beneficial to both races, Maori and Pakeha, and to the future of New Zealand as a society. They also highlight the fact that, despite the vociferousness of extremists or radical camps of whatever race, the present generation of Maori and Pakeha have a task of paramount importance to them and to posterity—to salvage and fuse what is useful from Maori culture to European culture, and vice-versa, and to re-form the colonialist political and social heritage in a way that redresses certain undeniable past injustices and yet curbs the apparent selfishness of a few. If the present generation refuses to address, now, the issues that these writings highlight, they cannot avert the inter-cultural dislocation that is their inheritance and which will in turn be the lot of both their children and future generations.

BIBLIOGRAPHY

Primary Sources

Ihimaera, Witi. *Maori.* Wellington: A. R. Shearer, Govt. Printer, 1975.

—. *The Matriarch.* Auckland: Heinemann, 1986.

—. *The New Net Goes Fishing.* 1977. Auckland: Heinemann, 1981.

—. *Pounamu, Pounamu.* 1972. Auckland: Heinemann, 1974.

—. *Tangi.* 1973. Auckland: Heinemann, 1975.

—. *The Whale Rider.* Auckland: Heinemann, 1987.

—. *Whanau.* 1974. Auckland: Heinemann, 1983.

Ihimaera, Witi, and D. S. Long, eds. *Into the World of Light: an Anthology of Maori Writing.* Auckland: Heinemann, 1982.

Orbell, Margaret, ed. *Contemporary Maori Writing.* Wellington: Reed, 1970.

O'Sullivan, Vincent, ed. *New Zealand Short Stories.* Oxford: Oxford UP, 1975.

Shadbolt, Maurice. *Season of the Jew.* London: Hodder and Stoughton, 1986.

Secondary Sources

Books

Achebe, Chinua. *Morning Yet on Creation Day*. London: Heinemann, 1975.

Bassett, Judith, Keith Sinclair, and Marcia Stenson. *The Story of New Zealand*. Auckland: Reed Methuen Publishers, 1985.

Cook, David. *African Literature: A Critical View*. London: Longman, 1977.

Corballis, Richard, and Simon Garrett. *Introducing Witi Ihimaera*. Auckland: Longman Paul, 1984.

Curnow, Wystan, ed. *Essays on New Zealand Literature*. Auckland: Heinemann, 1973.

Jones, Lawrence. *Barbed Wire & Mirrors: Essays on New Zealand Prose*. 2nd ed. Dunedin: University of Otago Press, 1990.

McKenzie, D. F. *Oral Culture, Literacy and Print in Early New Zealand*. Wellington: Victoria University Press, 1985.

Pearson, Bill. *Fretful Sleepers and Other Essays*. London: Heinemann, 1974.

Schwimmer, Erik Gabriel. *The Maori People in the Nineteen-Sixties*. (with the cooperation of John Forster, William Parker, and James E. Ritchie) Auckland: Blackwood and Janet Paul Ltd, 1968.

Smith, Rowland, ed. *Exile and Tradition*. New York: Africana Publishing Company, 1976.

Soyinka, Wole. *Myth, Literature and the African World*. London: Cambridge University Press, 1976.

Stevens, Joan. *The New Zealand Novel 1860–1965*. 1961. 2nd ed. Wellington: A. H. and A. W. Reed, 1966.

Walsh, William. *Commonwealth Literature*. Oxford: Oxford University Press, 1973.

Walshe, R. D. ed. *Speaking of Writing*. Sydney: Reed Education, 1975.

Articles and Reviews

Alcock, C. M. Peter. "Informing the Void: Initial Cultural Displacement in New Zealand Writing." *Journal of Commonwealth Literature* 6.1 (1971): 84–102.

Arvidson, K. O. "Emergence of a Polynesian Literature." *World Literature Written in English* 14.1 (1975): 91–116.

—. Review of *The New Net Goes Fishing*, by Witi Ihimaera. *New Zealand Bookworld* Nov. 1977: 20.

Beckmann, Susan. "Language as Cultural Identity in Achebe, Ihimaera, Laurence and Atwood." *World Literature Written in English* 20.1 (1981): 117–34.

Beston, B. John. "The Fiction of Patricia Grace." *Ariel* 15.2 (1984): 41–53.

—. "Interview With Witi Ihimaera." *World Literature Written in English* 16.1 (Apr. 1977): 115–25.

—. "Two Responses: II." Review of *The Matriarch*, by Witi Ihimaera. *Landfall* 41.1 (1987): 84–6.

—. "Witi Ihimaera, Maori Novelist in a Changing Society." *Commonwealth* 3 (1977/78): 19–28.

Blank, Arapera. "Last and Best." Review of *Potiki*, by Patricia Grace. *New Zealand Listener* 15 Mar. 1986: 31.

Caffin, Elizabeth. "*The Matriarch*: Two Views 1: a Fictional Performance." Review of *The Matriarch*, by Witi Ihimaera. *New Zealand Listener* 16–22 Aug. 1986: 52–5.

Calder, Alex. "Two Responses: I." Review of *The Matriarch*, by Witi Ihimaera. *Landfall* 41.1 (1987): 79–84.

Corballis, Richard. "Witi Ihimaera: Literary Diplomacy." *Landfall* 33 (1979): 64–71.

Corrigan, Diane and Pat Hohepa. "Death of an Honorary White: [Interview with Atareta Poananga]." *Broadsheet* 148 (Apr. 1987): 13–9.

Dryland, Gordon. Review of *Whanau*, by Witi Ihimaera. *Thursday* 30 Jan. 1975: 52.

Durix, J. P. "Time in Witi Ihimaera's Tangi." *Journal of New Zealand Literature* 1 (1983): 101–14.

Farach, Anne Lee. "Powerful and Tender." Review of *The Matriarch*, by Witi Ihimaera. *PSA Journal* 18 Jun.–15 Jul. 1986: 17.

Fox, Alistair. "In Search of the Emerald City: the Short Stories of Witi Ihimaera." *Pilgrims* (New Series) 8 (1980): 88–94.

Gibson, Colin. "Ambitous N.Z. Novel." Review of *The Matriarch*, by Witi Ihimaera. *Dunedin Star Weekender*, 7 Sept. 1986: 8.

Ihimaera, Witi. "The Maori Affairs Syndrome." Editorial. *New Zealand Listener* 27 Aug. 1977: 10.

—. "The Maori Landscape." Editorial. *New Zealand Listener* 30 Jul. 1977: 10.

—. "Maori Life and Literature: a Sensory Perception." *Turnbull Library Record* 15.1 (1982): 45–55.

—. "Te Taha Maori (The Other Side) Belongs to Us All." *New Zealand Bookworld* 2 (Jul. 1973): 3–6.

—. "Why I Write." *World Literature Written in English* 14.1 (1975): 117–9.

—. "A New/Old Collection." Review of *The House of the Talking Cat*, by J. C. Sturm. *New Zealand Listener* 17 Mar. 1984: 91–2.

Jones, Lawrence. "The One Story, Two Ways of Telling, Three Perspectives: Recent New Zealand Literary Autobiography." *Ariel* 16.4 (1985): 127–50, reprinted (and enlarged) in *Barbed Wire & Mirrors: Essays on New Zealand Prose.* 2nd ed. Dunedin: University of Otago Press, 1990.

Katene, Paul. Review of *Tangi*, by Witi Ihimaera. *Te Ao Hou* 75 (1974): 60.

King, Michael. "A Magnificent New Zealand-Baroque Near-Success." Review of *The Matriarch*, by Witi Ihimaera. *Metro* Aug. 1986: 170.

—. Review of *Whanau*, by Witi Ihimaera. *New Zealand Bookworld* 14 Feb. 1975: 24–5.

Lamb, Jonathan. "Problems of Originality: or, Beware of Pakeha baring Guilts." *Landfall* 40.3 (1986): 352–8.

Legat, Nicola. "Atareta Poananga and Te Ahi Kaa: What Do Maori Nationalists Want?" *Metro* 5.57 (Mar. 1986): 44–58.

Martin, M. S. "The Blending of Traditions: Witi Ihimaera's Contribution to New Zealand Literature." *International Fiction Review* 10.1 (1983): 53–5.

McEldowney, W. J. "Restoration of Pride." Review of *The Matriarch*, by Witi Ihimaera. *Otago Daily Times* 3 Sept. 1986: 30.

Mitcalfe, Barry. Review of *Tangi*, by Witi Ihimaera. *New Zealand Bookworld* 6 (1973): 16.

Murphy, Roy. "A Boy From Gisborne Pens a Success Story in the Big Apple: Reluctant Writer Comes of Age." Review of *The Matriarch*, by Witi Ihimaera. *Dominion Sunday Times* 7 Jul. 1987: 13.

Murton, J. Brian. "Waituhi: a Place in Maori New Zealand." *New Zealand Geographer* (Apr. 1979): 24–33.

Neill, Michael. "Coming Home: Teaching the Post-Colonial Novel." *Islands* 2 (1985): 38–53.

Niven, Alastair. "The Family in Modern African Literature." *Ariel* 12.3 (1981): 81–91.

Oppenheim, R. S. Review of *Pounamu, Pounamu*, by Witi Ihimaera. *Journal of the Polynesian Society* 84 (1975): 506–7.

Orbell, M. "Maori Women Writing: an Introductory Survey." *World Literature Written in English* 17.1 (1979): 252–6.

Parsonson, G. S. "The Road to Waitangi." (unpublished paper) History Department, University of Otago (Aug. 2, 1983).

Pearson, Bill. "Witi Ihimaera and Patricia Grace." *Critical Essays on the New Zealand Short Story*, ed. Cherry Hankin. Auckland: Heinemann, 1982. 166–84.

—. "The Maori and Literature: 1938–1965." *Essays on New Zealand Literature*, ed. Wystan Curnow. Auckland: Heinemann, 1973.

Piddington, K. and Witi Ihimaera. "New Zealand Foreign Policy: Choices, Challenges and Opportunities—Environment and Security." *New Zealand International Review* 9.5 (Sept/Oct. 1984): 12–5.

Poananga, Atareta. "The Matriarch: Takahia Wahine Toa—Trample on Strong Women: 1." Review of *The Matriarch*, by Witi Ihimaera. *Broadsheet* 145 (Dec. 1986): 24–8.

—. "The Matriarch: Takahia Wahine Toa—Trample on Strong Women: 2." Review of *The Matriarch*, by Witi Ihimaera. *Broadsheet* 146 (Jan.–Feb. 1987): 24–9.

Potiki, Janet. "*The Matriarch*: Two Views 2: a Dance with the Past." Review of *The Matriarch*, by Witi Ihimaera. *New Zealand Listener* 16–22 Aug. 1986: 52–5.

Rhodes, H. Winston. Review of *Tangi*, by Witi Ihimaera. *Landfall* 27.4 (1973): 348–51.

—. Review of *Whanau*, by Witi Ihimaera. *Landfall* 29.2 (1975): 161–4.

Riach, Alan. "Out of Africa." Review of *Six Plays*, by Wole Soyinka. *Landfall* 41.1 (1987): 77–9.

Schipper, Mineke. "Eurocentrism and Criticism: Reflections on the Study of Literature in Past and Present." *World Literature Written in English* 24.1 (1984): 16–27.

Simms, Norman. "A Maori Literature in English. Part 1: Prose Fiction—Patricia Grace." *Pacific Quarterly Moana* 3.2 (1978): 186–99.

—. "Maori Literature in English. Prose Writers. Part 2: Witi Ihimaera." *Pacific Quarterly Moana* 3.3 (1978): 336–48.

—. "Maori Literature in English: an Introduction." *World Literature Today* 52 (1978): 223–8.

—. Review of *The New Net Goes Fishing*, by Witi Ihimaera. *World Literature Today* 52 (1978): 696.

Simpson, Peter. "All in the Family: Continuum of Discourse in Recent New Zealand Criticism." *Ariel* 16.4 (1985): 3–26.

Stead, C. K. "War Book." Review of *The Matriarch*, by Witi Ihimaera. *London Review of Books* 18 Dec. 1986: 20–2.

Vincent, Rosemary. "Witi Ihimaera: Our Man in New York." *New Zealand Woman's Weekly* 17 Feb. 1986: 14–5.

Wall, Carroll. "Te Pakeha: the Search for White Identity." *Metro* (Aug. 1986): 35–48.

Wattie, Nelson. "The Community as Protagonist in the Novels of Chinua Achebe and Witi Ihimaera." *Individual and Community in Commonwealth Literature* ed. Daniel Massa. Malta: University Press, 1979. 69–74.

Wedde, Ian. Review of *The Matriarch*, by Witi Ihimaera. *Wellington City Magazine* Sept. 1986: 55.

Whaaga, Philip. Review of *The Matriarch*, by Witi Ihimaera. *Tu Tangata* Aug/ Sept. 1986: 31.

Wynn, G. "Tradition and Change in Recent Maori Fiction: the Writing of Witi Ihimaera." *International Fiction Review* 2 (1975): 127–31.

Young, David. "An End to the Silence." Review of *The Matriarch*, by Witi Ihimaera. *New Zealand Listener* 7 Jun. 1986: 24–5.

Zavros, Judy. "Witi Ihimaera: Big Tree or Just a Tall Spine?" *Thursday* 13 Mar. 1975: 22–3.

Notes

Foreword

1. Michael Neill, "Coming Home: Teaching the Post-colonial Novel," *Islands* 35 (April 1985), 39.
2. Patricia Grace, "Parade," *Waiariki* (Auckland: Longman Paul, 1975), p. 88.

Chapter 1: Ihimaera and the Maori Perspective

1. W. Pearson, "The Maori and Literature 1938–65," *The Maori People in the Nineteen-Sixties*, ed. Schwimmer, Erik Gabriel with the cooperation of John Forster et al., (Auckland: B. & J. Paul, 1968, i.e., 1969), pp. 217–56.
2. See Richard Corballis and Simon Garrett, *Introducing Witi Ihimaera*, (Auckland: Longman Paul, 1984), p. 10.
3. Bill Pearson, "Witi Ihimaera and Patricia Grace," *Critical Essays on New Zealand Short Story*, ed. Cherry Hankin, (Auckland: Heinemann, 1974), p. 167.
4. Richard Corballis and Simon Garrett, *Introducing Witi Ihimaera*, p. 10.
5. Ibid.
6. Witi Ihimaera, "Why I Write," *World Literature Written in English* 14.1 (1975), p. 118.
7. The phrase chosen by Witi Ihimaera and D. S. Long for the title of the anthology of Maori writing they edited in the early 1980s (Auckland: Heinemann, 1982).
8. John B. Beston, "Witi Ihimaera, Maori Novelist in a Changing Society," *Commonwealth* 3 (1977/78), p. 19.
9. Ibid.
10. Ibid.
11. Ibid.
12. Ibid., p. 20.
13. John B. Beston, "Interview with Witi Ihimaera," *World Literature Written in English* 16.1 (Apr. 1977), p. 120.
14. Bill Pearson, "Witi Ihimaera and Patricia Grace," *Critical Essays on the New Zealand Short Story*, p. 167.
15. Atareta Poananga, "*The Matriarch*: Takahia Wahine Toa—Trample on Strong Women, Part 1," Review of *The Matriarch*, by Witi Ihimaera, *Broadsheet* 145 (Dec. 1986), p. 26.

16. Nicola Legat, "Atareta Poananga and Te Ahi Kaa: What Do Maori Nationalists Want?" *Metro* 5.57 (Mar. 1986), p. 54.
17. Roy Murphy, "A Boy From Gisborne Pens a Success Story in the Big Apple: Reluctant Writer Comes of Age," *Dominion Sunday Times* (Jun. 7 1987), p. 13.
18. David Cook, *African Literature: A Critical View*, (London: Longman Group, 1977), p. 3.
19. Diane Corrigan and Pat Hohepa, "Death of an Honorary White: [Interview with Atareta Poananga]," *Broadsheet* 148 (Apr. 1987), p. 17.
20. Quoted by Roy Murphy, p. 13.
21. Witi Ihimaera, "Why I Write," *World Literature Written in English*, p. 118.
22. Witi Ihimaera, "Maori Life and Literature: a Sensory Perception," *Turnbull Library Record* 15.1 (May 1982), p. 53.
23. Witi Ihimaera, "Why I Write," *World Literature Written in English*, p. 117.
24. See Richard Corballis and Simon Garrett, *Introducing Witi Ihimaera*, p. 66.
25. Wellington: A. R. Sheerer, Govt Printer, 1975.
26. Co-edited with D. S. Long (Auckland: Heinemann, 1982). [Ten-years later, he selected and edited Vol. 1 of a further series, *Te Ao Marama: Contemporary Maori Writing* (Auckland, Reed Publishing (NZ) Ltd, 1992). — Ed.]
27. Roy Murphy, p. 13.

Chapter 2: From Pastoral to Political: A Changing Way of Life

1. Witi Ihimaera in his review of J. C. Sturm's collection of stories, *The House of the Talking Cat*, acknowledges that Sturm "began writing in the 1940s, was published in *Te Ao Hou* and *Numbers* in the 1950s, and achieved a *succes d'estime* in the 1960s when C. K. Stead chose one of her stories for *New Zealand Short Stories 2*." (*New Zealand Listener*, 17 Mar. 1984, pp. 91–2.) But Ihimaera was the first Maori to have a book of short stories published.
2. Roy Murphy, "A Boy From Gisborne Pens a Success Story in the Big Apple: Reluctant Writer Comes of Age," *Dominion Sunday Times* (7 Jun. 1987), p. 13.
3. Bill Pearson, "Witi Ihimaera and Patricia Grace," *Critical Essays on the New Zealand Short Story*, ed. Cherry Hankin, (Auckland: Heinemann, 1974), p. 166.

4. John B. Beston, "An Interview with Witi Ihimaera," *World Literature Written in English* 16.1 (Apr. 1977), p. 118.
5. Richard Corballis and Simon Garrett, *Introducing Witi Ihimaera*, (Auckland: Longman Paul, 1984), p. 16.
6. Ibid.
7. Witi Ihimaera, *The Matriarch*, p. 45.
8. Kinship and family responsibility; and reciprocal assistance to one another.
9. Richard Corballis and Simon Garrett, *Introducing Witi Ihimaera*, p. 17.
10. Richard Corballis and Simon Garrett, *Introducing Witi Ihimaera*, p. 22.
11. Chinua Achebe, "The Role of the Writer in a New Nation," *African Writers on African Writing*, ed. G. D. Killam, (Evanston: Northwestern U. P., 1973), p. 8.
12. Richard Corballis, "Witi Ihimaera: Literary Diplomacy," *Landfall* 33 (Mar. 1979), p. 66.
13. Ibid., p. 65.
14. John B. Beston, "Witi Ihimaera, Maori Novelist in a Changing Society," *Commonwealth* 3 (1977/78), p. 27.
15. John B. Beston, "An Interview with Witi Ihimaera," *World Literature Written in English*, p. 118.
16. Paul Katene, Review of *Tangi*, by Witi Ihimaera, *Te Ao Hou* 75 (Mar. 1974), p. 60.
17. Richard Corballis and Simon Garrett, *Introducing Witi Ihimaera*, p. 29.
18. Phrase borrowed from Soyinka's *Death and the King's Horseman*, (London: Eyre Methuen, 1975), p. 75.
19. Richard Corballis and Simon Garrett, *Introducing Witi Ihimaera*, p. 34 (my italics).
20. Ibid., pp. 34–5.
21. The kaumatua uses similar words—"Ae, even in his own day, Maoritanga had been dying"—and it's for the same reason that Tama gives for wanting to teach Maori traditional values to his younger brother and sister, that the kaumatua teaches Hera. ("The Whale," *Pounamu, Pounamu*, pp. 117–9).
22. Brian J. Murton, "Waituhi: a Place in Maori New Zealand," *New Zealand Geographer* 35. 1 (Apr. 1979), p. 30.
23. Ibid., p. 31.
24. Ibid.
25. Richard Corballis, "Witi Ihimaera: Literary Diplomacy," *Landfall*, p. 70.

26. Nelson Wattie, "The Community as Protagonist in the Novels of Chinua Achebe and Witi Ihimaera," *Individual and Community in Commonwealth Literature*, ed. Daniel Massa, (Malta: University Press, 1979), p. 72.
27. Ibo adage.
28. David Cook, *African Literature: a Critical View*, (London: Longman, 1977), pp. 3–4.
29. See Richard Corballis and Simon Garrett's analysis of Ihimaera's use of the kite as a linking device, in *Introducing Witi Ihimaera*, p. 39.
30. See Michael King, Review of *Whanau*, *New Zealand Bookworld* 14 (Feb. 1975), pp. 24–5.
31. Alistair Fox, "In Search of the Emerald City: the Short Stories of Witi Ihimaera," *Pilgrim* (New Series) 8 (Summer 1980), p. 91.
32. John B. Beston, "An Interview with Witi Ihimaera," *World Literature Written in English*, p. 122.
33. K. O. Arvidson, Review of *The New Net Goes Fishing*, by Witi Ihimaera, *New Zealand Bookworld* 42 (Nov. 1977), p. 20.
34. Carroll Wall, "Te Pakeha: the Search for White Identity," *Metro* (Aug. 1986), p. 36.
35. Biculturalism is implied by his father's comments about Matiu and his sister "making it" in the Pakeha world, and by Matiu's marriage to a Pakeha (which in Ihimaera's fiction is a symbol of the concept), but it is not categorically stated that that is what is in his mind.
36. Alistair Fox, "In Search of the Emerald City: the Short Stories of Witi Ihimaera," *Pilgrim*, p. 92.
37. Michael King, Review of *Whanau*, *NZ Bookworld*, pp. 24–5.
38. Ihimaera quoted in an interview with Roy Murphy, "A Boy From Gisborne" *Dominion Sunday Times*, p. 13.
39. Ibid.
40. Ibid.
41. Nicola Legat, "Atareta Poananga and Te Ahi Kaa: What do Maori Nationalists Want?" *Metro* 5. 57 (Mar. 1986), p. 56.
42. Corrigan, Diane, and Pat Hohepa, "Death of an Honorary White: [Interview with Atareta Poananga]," *Broadsheet* 148 (Apr. 1987), p. 17.
43. Nicola Legat, *Metro*, p. 56.
44. *Turnbull Library Record* 15.1 (1982), pp. 45, 49.
45. Witi Ihimaera, "The Maori Landscape," Editorial, *New Zealand Listener* (30 Jul. 1977), p. 10.
46. Ibid.

47. Ibid.
48. Witi Ihimaera, "Why I Write," *World Literature Written in English* 14.1 (1975), p. 117.

Chapter 3: Coming to Terms with the New Way: the Radicalisation of Ihimaera's Views in *The Matriarch*

1. Quoted by Alan Riach, Review of *Six Plays*, by Wole Soyinka, *Landfall* 41.1 (Mar. 1987), p. 79.
2. Bill Pearson, "Attitudes to the Maori in Some Pakeha Fiction," *Fretful Sleepers and Other Essays*, (Auckland: Heinemann, 1974), p. 46. (First published in the *Journal of the Polynesian Society*, Sept. 1958).
3. Ibid., p. 48.
4. Judith Bassett et al., *The Story of New Zealand*, (Auckland: Reed Methuen, 1985), p.28.
5. Lawrence Jones, *Barbed Wire & Mirrors: Essays on New Zealand Prose*, 2nd ed., (Dunedin: University of Otago Press, 1990), p. 313.
6. Judith Bassett et al., *The Story of New Zealand*, pp. 21–2.
7. Ibid., p. 35.
8. Ibid., pp. 35, 37.
9. [Dr Ojinmah's research was completed before the publication of the now well-known study—or group of studies—on the Treaty by Dr Claudia Orange—Ed.]
10. Ibid., pp. 42–3.
11. D. F. McKenzie, *Oral Culture, Literacy and Print in Early New Zealand*, (Wellington: Victoria University Press, 1985), p. 9.
12. Ibid.
13. Bassett et al., *The Story of New Zealand*, p. 47.
14. McKenzie, *Oral Culture, Literacy and Print in Early New Zealand*, p. 33.
15. Ibid.
16. Ibid.
17. Ibid., p. 35.
18. Ibid., p. 42.
19. Bassett et al., *The Story of New Zealand*, p. 45.
20. McKenzie, *Oral Culture, Literacy and Print in Early New Zealand*, p. 9.
21. Ibid., p. 10.
22. Ibid., p. 41.

23. Brian J. Murton's argument on this score is particularly perceptive:"Waituhi: a Place in Maori New Zealand," *New Zealand Geographer* 35.1 (1979), pp. 24–33.
24. See Richard Corballis and Simon Garrett, *Introducing Witi Ihimaera*, p. 66.
25. Gordon Parsonson, among others, argues that most of the lands in New Zealand did not actually "belong to" Maori, in the sense that Maori had never set foot on most of these lands; that it was the realisation of the economic value of land in the post-Pakeha period, and the subsequent wording of the Treaty of Waitangi, that have given rise to claims such as Ihimaera's. See his unpublished paper: "The Road to Waitangi," (2 Aug. 1983), courtesy of both Prof. Parsonson (for permission to use it) and Dr T. Brooking (for drawing my attention to it), History Department, University of Otago.
26. Brian J. Murton, "Waituhi: a Place in Maori New Zealand," *New Zealand Geographer*, pp. 31–2.
27. Maurice Shadbolt, *Season of the Jew*, (London: Hodder & Stoughton, 1986), p. 56.
28. Ibid.
29. Ibid., p. 93.
30. Ibid. (Note that Te Kooti and Coates refer to the same person and would be used interchangeably.)
31. Ibid., p. 92.
32. Ibid., p. 93.
33. Ibid., p. 62.
34. Ibid.
35. Ibid., pp. 81–2.
36. David Young, "An End to the Silence," Review of *The Matri arch*, by Witi Ihimaera, *New Zealand Listener* (7 Jun. 1986), p. 25.
37. Also, while Ihimaera's narration of this incident accounts for a small fraction of *The Matriarch*, Shadbolt's *Season of the Jew* is based entirely on the incident; his development of the theme is therefore much more detailed.
38. Roy Murphy, "A Boy from Gisborne Pens a Success Story in the Big Apple: Reluctant Writer Comes of Age," *The Dominion Sunday Times* (7 Jun. 1987), p. 13.
39. Ibid.
40. Bill Pearson, "Attitudes to the Maori in Some Pakeha Fiction", *Fretful Sleepers and Other Stories*, p. 48.

41. Witi Ihimaera, "Maori Life and Literature: a Sensory Perception," *Turnbull Library Record* 15.1 (May 1982), p. 54.
42. Witi Ihimaera and D. S. Long, "Contemporary Maori Writing: a Context," *Into the World of Light*, (Auckland: Heinemann, 1982), p. 2.
43. Witi Ihimaera, "Te Taha Maori (the Other Side) Belongs to Us All," *New Zealand Bookworld* 2 (Jul. 1973), p. 3.
44. Witi Ihimaera and D. S. Long, "Contemporary Maori Writing: a Context," *Into the World of Light*, p. 3.
45. *The Matriarch*, pp. 13, 17. She repeats the phrase "I have made him into a likeness as unto me", in various other forms.
46. C. K. Stead, "War Book," Review of *The Matriarch*, by Witi Ihimaera, *London Review of Books* (18 Dec. 1986), p. 20.
47. *The Matriarch*, p. 27. The similarity and usage of the phrase 'into . . . likeness' and the idea of bestriding both the Pakeha and the Maori worlds are consistent with the matriarch's intentions for Tamatea.
48. Janet Potiki, "A Dance With the Past," Review of *The Matriarch* by Witi Ihimaera, *New Zealand Listener* (16 Aug. 1986), p. 55.
49. Atareta Poananga, "*The Matriarch*: Takahia Wahine Toa— Trample On Strong Women, Part I," Review of *The Matriarch*, by Witi Ihimaera, *Broadsheet* 145 (Dec. 1986), p. 27.
50. Elizabeth Caffin, "A Fictional Performance," Review of *The Matriarch*, by Witi Ihimaera, *New Zealand Listener* (16 Aug. 1986), p. 52.
51. Ibid.
52. Janet Potiki, "A Dance With the Past," *Listener*, p. 55.
53. Atareta Poananga, *The Matriarch*: Review, *Broadsheet*, p. 26.
54. Corrigan, Diane, and Pat Hohepa, "Death of an Honorary White: [Interview with Atareta Poananga]," *Broadsheet* 148 (Apr. 1987), p. 17.

Chapter 4: Myth and Modern Reality: the Dilemma of Biculturalism in Ihimaera's Recent Fiction

1. Richard Corballis and Simon Garrett, *Introducing Witi Ihimaera*, p. 22.
2. Ibid.
3. Ihimaera also likens Koro Apirana to a stranded whale: "Our Koro was like an old whale stranded in an alien present, but

that was how it was supposed to be because he also had his role in the pattern of things, in the tide of the future." (*The Whale Rider*, p. 59)

4. Richard Corballis and Simon Garrett, *Introducing Witi Ihimaera*, p. 22.
5. *The Matriarch*, pp. 280–427.
6. K. Piddington and Witi Ihimaera, "Environment, Security and Identity: a 'maui-esque' viewpoint," *New Zealand International Review* 9.5 (Sept.–Oct. 1984), p. 14.
7. Ibid.
8. Atareta Poananga, "*The Matriarch*: Takahia Wahine Toa—Trample On Strong Women, Part I", Review of *The Matriarch*, by Witi Ihimaera, *Broadsheet* 145 (Dec. 1986), p. 27.
9. Witi Ihimaera, "Maori Life and Literature: a Sensory Perception," *Turnbull Library Record* 15.1 (May 1982), pp. 53–4.
10. John B. Beston, "An Interview with Witi Ihimaera," *World Literature Written in English* 16.1 (1977), p. 120.
11. Alistair Fox, "In search of the Emerald City: the Short Stories of Witi Ihimaera," *Pilgrim* (New Series) 8 (Summer 1980), p. 88.
12. John B. Beston, "An Interview with Witi Ihimaera," p. 122.
13. Feature, "Helping to Foster Te Manaaki—Witi wants to Share the Sharing," *New Zealand Bookworld* 2 (Jul. 1973), p. 1.
14. Ibid.
15. Atareta Poananga, *The Matriarch*: Review, *Broadsheet*, p. 26.
16. Ibid.
17. Witi Ihimaera, "The Maori Landscape," Editorial, *New Zealand Listener* (30 Jul. 1977), p. 10.
18. Ibid.
19. Witi Ihimaera and D. S. Long, Introduction, *Into the World of Light*, p. 3.
20. Nicola Legat, "Atareta Poananga and Te Ahi Kaa: What do Maori Nationalists Want?" *Metro*, p. 46.
21. Witi Ihimaera, "The Maori Landscape," Editorial, *New Zealand Listener* (30 Jul. 1977), p. 10.
22. Roy Murphy, "A Boy from Gisborne Pens a Success Story in the Big Apple: Reluctant Writer Comes of Age," *Dominion Sunday Times*, p. 13.
23. Witi Ihimaera, "Maori Life and Literature: a Sensory Perception," *Turnbull Library Record*, p. 47. (my italics)

Chapter 5: Conclusion

1. Witi Ihimaera, "Why I Write," *World Literature Written in English* 14.1 (Apr. 1975), p. 118.
2. John B. Beston, "An Interview with Witi Ihimaera," *World Literature Written in English* 16.1 (Apr. 1977), p. 117.
3. Ibid.
4. Witi Ihimaera, "Why I Write," *World Literature Written in English*, p. 117.
5. Witi Ihimaera, "Maori Life and Literature: a Sensory Perception," *Turnbull Library Record*, p. 53.
6. Ibid.
7. Nicola Legat, "Atareta Poananga and Te Ahi Kaa—What Do Maori Nationalists Want?" *Metro* 5.57 (Mar. 1986), p. 54.
8. Ibid.
9. Roy Murphy, "A Boy From Gisborne Pens a Success Story in the Big Apple: Reluctant Writer Comes of Age," *Dominion Sunday Times* (Jun. 7 1987), p. 13.

INDEX

Maori words are italicised here, and to assist in the pronunciation of words that have not entered New Zealand English, macrons are used in preference to the double vowel. Brief, simplified meanings are offered; for fuller meanings it is preferable to consult a good dictionary, such as H. W. Williams's *Dictionary of the Maori Language*, 7th ed. 1971 (Wellington: GP Publications, 6th reprinting, 1992).